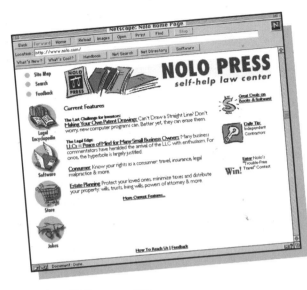

FIRST EDITION

9 Ways to Avoid Estate Taxes

by attorneys
Denis Clifford and Mary Randolph

NOLO PRESS BERKELEY

YOUR RESPONSIBILITY WHEN USING A SELF-HELP LAW BOOK

We've done our best to give you useful and accurate information in this book. But this book does not take the place of a lawyer licensed to practice law in your state. If you want legal advice, see a lawyer. If you use any information contained in this book, it's your personal responsibility to make sure that the facts and general information contained in it are applicable to your situation.

KEEPING UP-TO-DATE

To keep its books up-to-date, Nolo Press issues new printings and new editions periodically. New printings reflect minor legal changes and technical corrections. New editions contain major legal changes, major text additions or major reorganizations. To find out if a later printing or edition of any Nolo book is available, call Nolo Press at (510) 549-1976 or check the catalog in the *Nolo News*, our quarterly newspaper, or online at www.nolo.com.

To stay current, follow the "Update" service in the *Nolo News*. You can get a free one-year subscription by sending us the registration card in the back of the book. In another effort to help you use Nolo's latest materials, we offer a 25% discount off the purchase of the new edition of your Nolo book when you turn in the cover of an earlier edition. For details, see the back of this book.

FIRST EDITION	**January 1999**
PRODUCTION	Sarah Toll
EDITOR	Ralph Warner and Shae Irving
PROOFREADER	Joe Sadusky
INDEX	Jane Meyerhofer
PRINTING	Bertelsmann Industry Services
COVER	Toni Ihara

Clifford, Denis.
    9 ways to avoid estate taxes / by Denis Clifford and Mary Randolph.
        p. cm.
    Includes index.
    ISBN 0-87337-466-5
    1. Inheritance and transfer tax--Law and legislation--United States--Popular works. I. Randolph, Mary. II. Title.
    KF6585.C583 1998
    343.7305'32--dc21   98-36075
                                      CIP

Acknowledgments

We would like to thank our two Nolo editors: Jake Warner, who challenged us with his questions, and Shae Irving, who gave the manuscript a sharp and careful final going-over. Both left the book vastly better than they found it.

Thanks also to two other Nolo authors whose expertise found their way into this book: tax attorney Fred Daily, author of *Tax Savvy for Small Business*, and Cora Jordan, attorney, mediator and co-author of *Plan Your Estate*.

About the Author's

Denis Clifford is a lawyer who specializes in estate planning. He is the author of several Nolo Press books, including *Plan Your Estate*, *Make Your Own Living Trust* and *Nolo's Will Book*. A graduate of Columbia Law School, where he was an editor of *The Law Review*, he has practiced law in various ways, and became convinced that people can do much of the legal work they need themselves.

Mary Randolph gave up the practice of law to write and edit Nolo Press books, and has never regretted it for a minute. She received her law degree from Boalt Hall, the law school at the University of California at Berkeley. She is the author of the *Living Trust Maker* legal manual, *The Deeds Book*, *8 Ways to Avoid Probate* and *Dog Law*, also published by Nolo Press.

ICONS USED IN THIS BOOK

 CAUTION: A potential problem.

FAST TRACK: Lets you know that you may be able to skip some material.

 RESOURCE: Refers you to another self-help resource.

LAWYER: Situations when you should see a lawyer about a particular issue.

 TIP: A bit of advice that may help you with a particular issue.

CONTENTS

INTRODUCTION

UNDERSTANDING THE FEDERAL GIFT AND ESTATE TAX

CHAPTER 1

MAKE GIFTS UNDER $10,000

CHAPTER 2

PAY TUITION OR MEDICAL EXPENSES

CHAPTER 3

LEAVE OR GIVE PROPERTY TO YOUR SPOUSE

CHAPTER 4

USE A BYPASS (AB) TRUST

CHAPTER 5

USE A QTIP TRUST

CHAPTER 6

GIVE TO CHARITY

CHAPTER 7

TRANSFER OWNERSHIP OF YOUR LIFE INSURANCE POLICIES

CHAPTER 8

USE DISCLAIMERS

CHAPTER 9

USE SPECIAL RULES FOR SMALL BUSINESSES

GLOSSARY

INTRODUCTION

Understanding the Federal Gift and Estate Tax

If you are concerned about estate tax, consider yourself lucky. You may not think of yourself as wealthy, but you belong to the small percentage of Americans who have enough money to interest the federal estate tax authorities.

Estate tax, as you probably know, is a tax levied on the property a person leaves at death. Only a fraction of estates—the largest ones—must pay estate tax each year. For someone who dies in 1999, estate tax may be due only if the value of the taxable estate exceeds $650,000. That threshold will rise to $1 million by 2006. And the many exemptions to estate tax (discussed in this chapter and throughout the book) make it possible for many people to transfer much larger estates without owing tax.

THE FEDERAL GIFT/ESTATE TAX THRESHOLD

Year of Death	Amount You Can Give Away or Leave Without Owing Tax
1999	$650,000
2000-2001	$675,000
2002-2003	$700,000
2004	$850,000
2005	$950,000
2006 and after	$1 million

ESTATE PLANNING: A PROCESS, NOT AN EVENT

As you ponder the tax-planning techniques in this book, keep in mind that what's best for you and your family will undoubtedly change over the years. You can't expect to make one plan when you're in your 50s that will carry you through to old age and all the changes life brings. The best rule? Keep it simple when you're young, and explore more complex options as you get older.

A. The Unified Gift and Estate Tax: An Overview

The federal estate tax you've heard about is actually something called the "unified gift and estate tax." The difference is more than semantic. There really is just one tax, applied to large gifts made during life and large estates left at death.

In an effort to tax transfers of wealth the same way whether they are made before or after death, gift and estate tax rates are identical. Currently, they start at 37% and go up to a whopping 55%—making it worthwhile to avoid them if possible.

The reason most people never owe gift/estate tax is that everyone can give away or leave a certain amount (listed above) without owing any gift or estate tax at all. That amount is commonly called the "estate tax threshold," the "exempt amount" or the "personal estate tax exemption."

Gift/estate tax must be paid if and when:

- During your life, you use up your entire exempt amount ($650,000 to $1 million, depending on the year) by making taxable gifts. This is rare, partly because few people have that kind of money to give away and partly because most gifts aren't taxable (see Section B, below); or

- At your death, the value of the taxable property you leave behind (not all property is taxable, as discussed in Section C, below), plus taxable gifts you made during life, is more than the exempt amount in the year of your death.

This means that to plan wisely to reduce estate tax, you should decide whether or not you want to make large gifts during your life. If you do, you'll also want to figure out how your gift-giving could affect your personal estate tax exemption.

Example 1: *Jonas makes $300,000 in taxable gifts during his lifetime. Because his gifts total less than the exempt amount, he doesn't have to pay gift tax. At his death, he leaves another $350,000 to friends. He dies in 2002, when the exempt amount is $700,000. Because the total amount he transferred (before and after death) is $650,000, his estate owes no estate tax.*

Example 2: *Margaret, who is both wealthy and generous, decides to give away much of her money before her death. She starts her gift-giving in 2003; five years later, she has made large, taxable gifts that add up to $1 million. Because she has used up her personal exemption from estate tax ($1 million in 2006), she must pay tax on all future taxable gifts made during her life. When she dies in 2010, leaving an estate worth $500,000, nothing is left of her personal estate tax exemption. Her estate must pay tax on the entire $500,000.*

Example 3: *Perry makes taxable gifts of $50,000 during his life. When he dies in 2004, he leaves property worth $900,000 to his children. The exempt amount for that year is $850,000. Because he has used up $50,000 of the exemption, $800,000 remains. His estate will owe estate tax on $100,000.*

> ### WHY DEATH TAXES?
>
> Whether or not to tax property transferred at death is a decision that every society makes. In the days of 19th-century "survival of the fittest" capitalism, there were no federal estate taxes. Modern America taxes the estates of only its wealthiest citizens. Some European countries claim larger portions of big estates.

B. Gift Tax

Many affluent people give away property during their lives so that when they die, there will be less property subject to estate tax. But how does that work, given that gift and estate tax rates are the same? The answer is that many, probably most, gifts are exempt from gift tax. Once you know how to make tax-free gifts, you can easily, legally and substantially reduce the size of your taxable estate .

1. Which Gifts Are Taxed and Which Are Not

All of these gifts are **exempt** from gift tax:

- Gifts worth less than $10,000 per recipient in one calendar year.
- Gifts of any amount to your spouse, if he or she is a U.S. citizen.
- Gifts of up to $100,000 per year to your spouse, if he or she is **not** a U.S. citizen.
- Gifts of any amount made in direct payment of someone's medical bills or tuition.

The $10,000 exemption (called the "annual exclusion" by the IRS) is the most important one for most people. It lets you give any number of recipients up to $10,000 each in any calendar year, completely tax-free.

Couples can combine their exemptions and give each recipient up to $20,000 yearly.

If you make a gift that does not fall into any of the tax-exempt categories, you are required by law to file a federal gift tax return with the IRS. The amount of the taxable gift uses up some of your gift/estate tax exemption. You don't actually have to pay tax, however, unless and until you use up the entire exemption amount. (See section 3, below.)

Example: *Alicia gives her daughter $45,000 for the down payment on a house. Alicia must file a federal gift tax return, reporting the taxable portion of the gift, $35,000. (The first $10,000 is completely tax-exempt.) She has used up $35,000 of her gift/estate tax exemption, but she doesn't owe the IRS any money right now.*

Alicia dies in 2002, when the gift/estate tax exemption amount is $700,000. Because of the $35,000 taxable gift she made several years earlier, only $665,000 of the exempt amount is still available to her estate. If her estate is less than that amount, it won't owe any estate tax.

WHO PAYS GIFT TAX?

Federal gift tax is assessed against someone who gives a gift, not the recipient. The recipient must foot the bill only if the giver fails to pay any tax actually due.

---

2. Gift Tax Returns

If you must file a federal gift tax return (IRS Form 709 or 709-A), it is due when your regular income tax return is filed—for most folks, April 15. You are required to file a return if, during the previous tax year, you:

- made non-exempt gifts, or
- made gifts to a tax-exempt organization over the amount of the annual exclusion, if you gave less than your entire interest in the

property. No tax is assessed for these tax-exempt gifts, but the IRS still insists on a return.

Similarly, no return is required for gifts for educational or medical expenses, no matter how large. (To be sure that gifts you make for these purposes are tax-exempt, see Chapter 2.) And you never need to file a gift tax return for gifts to your spouse, if he or she is a United States citizen; all these gifts are tax-exempt. If your spouse is not a citizen, and the gift exceeds $100,000 in one year, the gift is not exempt, and a return is required.

3. Gift Tax Payments

If you make a taxable gift and file a gift tax return, the IRS will assess gift tax against you. But, as mentioned earlier, you don't have to pay the tax when it's assessed. As a matter of fact, you can't pay now even if you would like to. In other words, you cannot choose to pay the gift tax now and save all of your personal exemption for later use. Instead, the amount of the gift always reduces the amount of your personal gift/estate tax exemption.

Example: *Amber gives Beatrice an expensive car, worth $50,000. Gift tax is assessed on $40,000, the amount by which the gift exceeds the $10,000 annual gift tax exclusion. Amber cannot simply pay the amount of the tax now and preserve the full amount of her personal gift/estate tax exemption for her estate to use after her death. The IRS requires that she use up $40,000 of her personal exemption.*

Your estate may not ever have to pay the gift tax that is assessed while you are alive.

Example: *Let's continue the previous example. When Amber dies in 2003, she leaves $500,000 in taxable assets. That means she's used up a total of $540,000 (her $500,000 estate plus the $40,000 taxable gift of the car) of her* *personal gift/estate tax exemption, which in 2003 is $700,000. Her estate owes no tax.*

At Amber's Death in 2002:

Taxable estate	*$500,000*
Taxable gift during life	*+$40,000*
Net taxable estate	*$540,000*

4. Gift and Estate Tax Rates

The gift/estate tax rates are graduated, so the higher the taxable value of the gift, the higher the gift tax rate that applies to it. Also, the tax rate is cumulative. This means that in determining the gift tax rate applied to a current gift, the value of all previous taxable gifts (made since January 1, 1977) must be taken into account. Otherwise, large estates could be transferred at lower tax rates by piecemeal giving.

Example 1: *By 2006, Wally has given his children a total of $1.1 million in taxable gifts.. Wally must pay gift tax on the $100,000 that exceeds the personal gift/estate tax exemption (in 2006) of $1 million. The tax will be $41,000.*

Example 2: *Wally gives his children a total of $200,000 in taxable gifts during his life. He dies in 2006, leaving $900,000 in taxable assets. Adding the taxable gifts to the $900,000 estate gives Wally a taxable estate of $1.1 million. The personal gift/estate tax exemption in 2006 is $1 million. Wally's estate owes tax on the $100,000 excess. The tax will be $41,000.*

C. Federal Estate Tax

After a death, if the gross value of the estate—that is, the value of everything the person owned, not taking into account mortgages or other debts owed on the property—exceeds the estate tax threshold, an estate tax return must be filed. But just because a return is filed doesn't mean there will be tax to pay.

1. What Is Taxed and What Isn't

Depending on your circumstances, much of your property may not be subject to estate tax. Here are the most important federal estate tax exemptions:

- **The personal estate tax exemption,** which allows a set dollar amount of property to pass tax-free, no matter who inherits it. (IRC § 2010.) The amount depends on the year of death.

YEAR OF DEATH	PERSONAL EXEMPTION AMOUNT
1999	$650,000
2000-2001	$675,000
2002-2003	$700,000
2004	$850,000
2005	$950,000
2006 and after	$1 million

- **The marital deduction,** which exempts from estate tax *all* property left to a surviving spouse who is a United States citizen. (IRC § 2056(a).) Property left to a non-citizen spouse is not exempt. (See Chapter 3 for ideas on leaving property to a non-citizen spouse.)

⚠ The marital deduction can be a tax trap. *If you leave your spouse a substantial amount of property, and he or she doesn't live long enough to spend it, you can inadvertently cause estate tax problems down the line. That's because your spouse's estate, increased by what you've left him or her, may go over the estate tax threshold. Chapter 4 explains one way to sidestep this pitfall.*

- **The charitable deduction,** which exempts all property left to qualified tax-exempt charities. (See Chapter 6.)
- **The new family business exemption,** which under certain circumstances can exempt up to $1.3 million of your estate if the major asset is a family business. (See Chapter 9.)

2. Estate Tax Returns

An estate tax return (IRS Form 706) must be filed for any estate with a gross value exceeding the amount of the personal exemption for the year of death. That's *gross* value (total value of the property), not net (value of your equity in the property). This means that your executor may have to file an estate tax return even though no taxes are actually due.

Example: *Dan's estate consists of $100,000 in cash, household goods, life insurance, a car and other items worth $50,000, and two houses, both heavily mortgaged.*

Here are the gross and net estate figures:

	Gross Value	Net Value (Equity)
Cash:	*$100,000*	*$100,000*
Personal property:	*$50,000*	*$50,000*
Life insurance:	*$200,000*	*$200,000*
House 1:	*$300,000*	*$150,000*
House 2:	*$200,000*	*$100,000*
Total	*$850,000*	*$600,000*

Dan dies in 2003, when the personal estate tax exemption is $700,000. Because Dan's gross estate exceeds this amount, his executor must see that an estate tax return is filed. But because his net estate is well under this amount, no tax will be due.

If an estate tax return must be filed, it's due within nine months of the death. The IRS commonly grants requests for extensions.

The executor of the deceased person's will is legally responsible for filing an estate tax return, if one is due. If there is no will, but there is a living trust, the job falls to the successor trustee named in the trust.

In perhaps the most common situation, a person creates both a will and living trust and names the same person to serve as executor and successor trustee. If, in unusual circumstances, the executor and successor trustee are not the same person, they must cooperate. The executor needs enough financial information to determine whether an estate tax return need be filed, and if so, what the right figures are.

Filing a return. *If a federal estate tax return must be filed, the executor will probably want to hire a tax expert. Form 706 is a long, very complicated form.*

3. The Estate Tax Credit

Most discussions of estate tax (including this one) talk about the $650,000-to-$1 million personal estate tax "exemption." That's a perfectly good way of thinking about gift/estate taxes, because you can leave that much property tax-free. But the tax law actually talks in terms of tax credits, not exempt amounts of property. If you want to know how the federal estate tax credit actually works, read on. If not, it's fine to keep thinking and planning in terms of the "exempt amount" you can leave or give away tax-free.

The tax law does not say that everyone who dies, say, in 2002 can give away or leave $700,000 tax-free. Instead, it says that someone who dies then gets a credit against gift/estate tax that is equal to the tax on $700,000. It all amounts to the same thing. But when an estate tax return is actually filed, the distinction becomes important, because first the tax must be computed, and then the credit is subtracted.

BAD NEWS FOR THE VERY RICH

Estates worth more than $10 million don't get the full gift/estate tax credit, and there is no credit at all for estates exceeding $24,100,000. The people who inherit these estates will just have to manage somehow.

UNIFIED GIFT/ESTATE TAX CREDIT

Year of Death	Estate Tax Credit	Equal to Tax on:
1999	$211,300	$650,000
2000-2001	$220,550	$675,000
2002-2003	$229,800	$700,000
2004	$287,300	$850,000
2005	$326,300	$950,000
2006 and after	$345,800	$1 million

As an example, here is how the calculations would be made for estates of $790,000 in 1999 and in 2006, when the credit will be higher.

ESTATE TAX ON NET TAXABLE ESTATE OF $790,000

	Death in 1999	Death in 2006
Tax assessed:	$263,900	$263,900
Estate tax credit:	($211,300) [equal to tax due on $650,000]	($345,800) [equal to tax due on $1 million]
Estate tax due:	= $52,600	= $0

If you want to know how to figure out the amount of estate tax assessed, see Section D.3, below.

D. Will Your Estate Have to Pay Taxes?

Even if you leave a lot of property, tax law exemptions and deductions may whittle the size of your taxable estate down below the exempt amount. The tax bill depends on some other factors, too: who inherits your property, and when you die.

1. Estimating Your Net Worth

You can't, of course, know what the value of your estate will be at your death. The best you can do is make a sensible estimate of your current net worth—that is, assets minus liabilities. This should be sufficient for estate tax planning purposes. If you're near or over the estate tax threshold now, your estate will probably owe tax at your death.

To help you make a good guess, check the list of common kinds of valuable property, below. You may want to jot down what you own and what you think each item is worth.

VALUABLE PROPERTY

Animals
Antiques
Appliances
Art
Books
Cameras
Cash accounts (CDs, savings, checking, money market)
Coins, stamps
Computers
Copyrights, patents, trademarks
Electronics
Furniture
Jewelry
Life insurance (proceeds that will be paid at your death)
Money owed to you
Precious metals
Real estate
Retirement accounts
Royalties
Small business ownership interests
Stocks, bonds and other securities
Tools
Vehicles

To make an estimate, for most items you can use the current market value of the property, less any debts on it. There is one important exception to this rule: For estate tax purposes, real estate used for a family business or farm can be valued for its continued use as a farm or business, not at its highest possible market value. So even if farmland would be worth more if it were sold to a developer to build a shopping center, you don't have to use that higher value.

If you're not sure how to value some types of property, such as royalty rights or stock in a closely held corporation, make your best guess. If you really have no idea of what something's worth, but you're sure it's quite valuable, you may want to get an expert appraiser's opinion. Unless you are elderly or ill, however, it's rarely necessary to pay for an appraisal at this stage in the planning process.

APPRAISALS AFTER YOUR DEATH

After your death, it will probably be necessary to put a more precise value on the worldly goods you've left behind. The person who winds up your affairs will have the responsibility of getting your property appraised, if it's necessary for tax or probate purposes. The federal government isn't involved in the appraisal, but the IRS can audit estate tax returns and challenge appraisals it thinks questionable.

To help an appraiser establish the market value of difficult-to-value items—works of art, small family businesses or stock in small corporations, for example—it's a good idea to save receipts, bookkeeping records and other documents that state the actual cost of items.

If an estate tax return must be filed, the executor of the estate has a choice when it comes to valuing the property in the estate. It can be valued as of the date of death, or six months afterwards (in tax lingo, the "alternate valuation date"). Which date is more advantageous depends on the situation. For example, if someone died owning a million dollars' worth of real estate, and then property values suddenly crashed in the area, using the six-months-later date could save a bundle on taxes.

---

2. Excluding Property That Isn't Subject to Estate Tax

Once you've got a rough estimate of what your property is worth, subtract everything that falls into the tax-exempt categories discussed above:

- All property you plan to leave to your spouse, if he or she is a United States citizen.

- All property you plan to leave to a tax-exempt charity.

You can also subtract your estimates of other deductible expenses, including last illness and funeral expenses, probate fees, any creditors' claims against your estate and death taxes paid to the state or foreign countries. But for most people, these exemptions are relatively minor.

Also remember to add back into your estate the value of any taxable gifts you've made (or expect to make) during your life.

ESTIMATING YOUR TAXABLE ESTATE	
Gross value of estate	$_____
Property left to spouse	($_____)
Property left to tax-exempt charities	($_____)
Net value of estate	= $_____
Taxable gifts made during life	+ $_____
Taxable estate	= $_____

3. Estimating the Tax Due

Most people don't bother trying to figure out just how much estate tax their estates will eventually owe. After all, the size of your estate will surely change by the time you die, and you don't know how large the exempt amount will be at the year of death. Just as Congress raised the amounts in 1997, it may do so again.

Especially if you are in your 50s or 60s and can expect to live several more decades, it makes more sense to concentrate on using the methods discussed in this book to bring the size of your estate down below the estate tax threshold. But if you want to run some numbers, to get some idea of just how much money your family can save if you do take steps to minimize estate taxes, here's how to proceed.

First, understand that the tax rate that applies depends on the entire value of the estate—not just the taxable amount. The lowest rate is a hefty 37% to 41%, depending on the year of death. The tax rate increases to 55% for estates over $3 million.

Example: *Joe dies in 2003 with an estate worth $800,000. In that year, $700,000 is exempt, so $100,000 of Joe's estate is subject to tax. But the tax rate applied to this amount is not the tax rate listed for $100,000; it's the rate for $800,000, which is 37%.*

To get an estimate of the tax that will be due, start with the estimate of your taxable estate from section 2, above. Then use the table below. It's a two-step process:

1. Based on the estimated size of your estate, figure the tentative tax.
2. Subtract the tax credit (Section C.3 above) for the estimated year of death.

THE ESTATE TAX BILL

If your taxable estate is:	The tentative tax (before subtracting the tax credit) will be:
$500,000 to $750,000	$155,800 plus 37% of amount over $500,000
$750,000 to $1 million	$248,300 plus 39% of amount over $750,000
$1 to $1.25 million	$345,800 plus 41% of amount over $1 million
$1.25 to $1.5 million	$448,300 plus 43% of amount over $1.25 million
$1.5 to $2 million	$555,800 plus 45% of amount over $1.5 million
$2 to $2.5 million	$780,000 plus 49% of amount over $2 million
$2.5 to $3 million	$1,025,800 plus 53% of amount over $2.5 million
More than $3 million	$1,290,800 plus 55% of amount over $3 million

Keep in mind that because you don't know what your estate will be worth when you die, let alone what year that will be, your results will be highly speculative.

Example 1: *Bernie estimates that he'll leave a net estate of $3 million to his children. The tentative tax on $3 million is $1,290,800. From this amount, he subtracts the unified tax credit for 2006 of $345,800. The estimated tax bill, if he dies in 2006 or after, is $945,000.*

Example 2: *Todd guesses he'll end up with a net estate worth $925,000, which he plans to leave equally to his friend Zeke and his sister Flo. Here is how he estimates the tax due.*

To begin, he figures the tentative tax due on $925,000:

Tentative tax on $750,000	$248,300
Tentative tax on $175,000 (39%)	+$68,250
Total tentative tax on $925,000	$316,550

Now that he's got the tentative tax figured, he can subtract the tax credit to which the estate will be entitled. For deaths in the year 2000, the unified gift/ estate tax credit will be $220,550. In 2005, the credit will be $326,300.

	Death in 2000	Death in 2005
Total tentative tax	$316,550	$316,550
Gift/estate tax credit	-$220,550	$326,300
Tax due	$96,000	-0-

More information on federal estate tax laws. *You can find more detailed information about these taxes in "Federal and Estate Gift Taxes," IRS Publication 448. It's available free at many IRS offices, or online at www.irs.ustreas.gov.*

E. State Gift and Death Taxes

For most people, state gift and estate taxes are minor matters, and don't enter into their estate planning. For that reason, we cover them only briefly. If you want to investigate them further, see a lawyer or contact your state's tax agency.

1. State Gift Taxes

Most states have no gift tax. Generally, when there is a state gift tax, its rules and rates are the same as those for the state's death tax.

STATES THAT IMPOSE GIFT TAX

Connecticut	North Carolina
Louisiana	South Carolina
New York	Tennessee
(repealed as of	
Jan. 1, 2000)	

---

2. State Death Taxes

Many states and the District of Columbia have effectively abolished state death taxes. The rest impose death taxes on:

- all real estate owned in the state, no matter where the deceased lived; and
- the personal property (everything but real estate) of residents of the state.

In many states, the bite taken from estates by state death taxes is annoying, but relatively minor. However, some states inflict more pain, especially when property is left to non-relatives. For example, Nebraska imposes only a 1% death tax rate if you leave $25,000 to your child, but 15% if you leave the money to a friend.

States follow one of three basic strategies when it comes to death taxes.

Pick-Up Taxes. Many states claim a share of the federal tax (if any) an estate owes, but don't impose any separate tax of their own. In those instances, a state death tax return must be filed (and there are penalties if it's not), but the state tax is taken out of what is owed the IRS. Your estate pays no additional taxes. This is commonly called a "pick-up" or "sop" death tax. In the table below, these states are listed as having effectively no estate tax.

Inheritance Taxes. Some states impose "inheritance" taxes on the recipients of inherited property, not the estate. Typically, states divide recipients into classes. For example, Class A may be just surviving husbands or wives. Class B may include immediate family—children and parents—and Class C may comprise brothers, sisters and cousins. Everyone else may be lumped in Class D. Each class receives different death tax exemptions and is taxed at a different rate. The general rule is that spouses pay little or no tax.

Estate Taxes. A few states impose a tax, like the federal one, on the taxable estate itself, without regard to who inherits the property.

SUMMARY OF STATE DEATH TAX RULES

State	Inheritance Tax?	Estate Tax?
Alabama	no	effectively, no
Alaska	no	effectively, no
Arizona	no	effectively, no
Arkansas	no	effectively, no
California	no	effectively, no
Colorado	no	effectively, no
Connecticut	yes, but phased out by 2005	no
Delaware	yes	no
District of Columbia	no	effectively, no
Florida	no	effectively, no
Georgia	no	effectively, no
Hawaii	no	effectively, no
Idaho	no	effectively, no
Illinois	no	effectively, no
Indiana	yes	effectively, no
Iowa	yes	effectively, no
Kansas	yes	effectively, no
Kentucky	yes	effectively, no
Louisiana	yes	effectively, no
Maine	no	effectively, no
Maryland	yes	effectively, no
Massachusetts	no	effectively, no
Michigan	yes	effectively, no
Minnesota	no	effectively, no
Mississippi	no	yes
Missouri	no	effectively, no
Montana	yes	effectively, no
Nebraska	yes	effectively, no
Nevada	no	effectively, no

New Hampshire	yes	effectively, no
New Jersey	yes	effectively, no
New Mexico	no	effectively, no
New York	no	yes, but repealed for people dying after Feb. 1, 2000
North Carolina	yes	yes
North Dakota	no	effectively, no
Ohio	no	yes
Oklahoma	no	yes
Oregon	no	effectively, no
Pennsylvania	yes	effectively, no
Rhode Island	no	effectively, no
South Carolina	no	effectively, no
South Dakota	yes	effectively, no
Tennessee	yes	effectively, no
Texas	no	effectively, no
Utah	no	effectively, no
Vermont	no	effectively, no
Virginia	no	effectively, no
West Virginia	no	effectively, no
Washington	no	effectively, no
Wisconsin	no	effectively, no
Wyoming	no	effectively, no

More information about state death taxes. Plan Your Estate, *by Denis Clifford and Cora Jordan (Nolo Press), contains detailed state-by-state information about death taxes. You may also be able to find information online if your state maintains a Web site.*

Make Gifts Under $10,000

One of the most popular ways to avoid estate tax is to give away property during your life. If you do so, you'll get more than just the benefit of reducing your survivors' estate tax burden. You'll also get to see the recipients enjoy your gifts.

Currently, you can make an unlimited number of $10,000 gifts of cash or other property each year, completely tax-free. If you made these same gifts after your death and they were subject to estate tax, the recipients would see their gifts shrink by at least 37%, the lowest estate tax rate now in effect. To ensure these tax savings, you need only remember that no individual recipient can receive more than $10,000 in a calendar year.

If you're comfortable giving away some of your wealth while you're alive, making $10,000 gifts is a fine way to remove property from your taxable estate. If you start soon enough, structure your gifts properly and watch the calendar, you can probably give away as much money or property as you want without worrying about tax.

Like all estate planning strategies, however, the decisions you must make about gift-giving are fundamentally personal. This chapter helps you evaluate whether giving away property is right for you and–if you decide to proceed—explains how to create a sound gift-giving program of your own.

GIFTS TO YOUR SPOUSE

All gifts that you make to your spouse are tax-free, as long as he or she is a U.S. citizen. If your spouse isn't a citizen, the limit on tax-free gifts is $100,000 per year. (26 U.S.C. § 2523(a).)

In practice, there's seldom a reason to make large gifts to your spouse. If you and your spouse each own about the same amount of property, you could actually worsen your tax situation by saddling your spouse with an estate that's so large it will be taxed at his or her death. (See Chapter 3.)

A. Thinking Before You Give

Gift-giving is such an easy and effective way to save on estate taxes that *Fortune* magazine once gushed that it was one of the "Three Things Everyone Should Do Now" to avoid taxes. (*"How to Leave the Tax Man Nothing,"* Mar. 18, 1996.) But an ambitious program of gift-giving is not for everyone.

Start with the obvious: When you give something away, it's gone forever. You can't change your mind. If parting with assets makes you feel vulnerable or nervous, fearful that you will someday be without money you need, don't do it. Another reason to hold off is that children or grandchildren may not be ready yet to handle or appreciate your generosity. You may not want your money spent on two weeks in Las Vegas or an expensive car.

For many people, however, especially as they get older, shedding material things brings a wonderful sense of lightness and freedom. Add to that the pleasure of seeing a younger relative, friend or organization benefit from a gift, and giving can return great satisfaction. Helping a 21-year-old get an education or the head of a new family buy a house may be a truly great gift.

One reason that planned gift-giving has gained in popularity is that people live so much longer than they used to. If you wait until you die to transfer your wealth, the recipients—for most people, their children—may be nearing old age themselves. Your financial help would probably have been much more useful when they were younger, struggling with house payments or scraping together the money for their children's orthodontia or college tuition.

These decisions are intensely personal. No formula (or lawyer) can tell you whether family members can handle large gifts or how much wealth you need to be comfortable in your own mind and heart. If you feel torn, it may help to sit down with pencil and paper (or computer) and make rough estimates of your current assets and future income and expenses, to get a clearer picture of your actual financial situation.

And remember that you don't need to make one big blockbuster gift. A series of relatively small gifts, made regularly to several beneficiaries, can remove a sizable amount of money from your taxable estate, while keeping you financially comfortable.

More information on assessing your financial situation. *For a sound discussion of how to estimate your retirement income and expenses realistically, see* Get a Life: You Don't Need a Million to Retire Well, *by Ralph Warner (Nolo Press).*

B. The $10,000 Annual Exclusion

The tax exemption that lets the first $10,000 you give to any person or non-charitable institution in a calendar year pass tax-free is called "the annual exclusion." (IRC § 2503(b).)

Despite the jargon, it's a pretty straightforward rule. If you give $25,000 to someone, $10,000 of it is exempt from gift tax. The remaining $15,000 is not. A few more examples:

- You give $8,000 to a cousin in one year: There are no federal gift tax consequences.
- You give $16,000 to your grandson in one year: $6,000 is subject to gift tax.

- You give $8,000 each to your two children: None of that $16,000 is subject to gift tax.

Beginning in 1999, the $10,000 exclusion amount is indexed for inflation; when the annual cost of living goes up $1,000, the exclusion amount will rise to $11,000. If inflation is 3% annually, it will take four years for the exclusion amount to tick up to $11,000.

 Gift Tax Basics. *For the basics on how gift tax is assessed and collected, see the introductory chapter of this book.*

1. Couples: Double Your Exclusion

Couples can combine their annual exclusions, which means that they can give away $20,000 of property tax-free, per year, per recipient. In fact, even if only one spouse makes a gift, it's considered to have been made by both spouses if they both consent. (IRC § 2513.) If a couple gives money to another couple, up to $40,000 can be transferred tax-free each year.

Example: *Joe and Faye, a couple in their late 70s, want to give their son and his wife money for a down payment on a house. They also see this as an opportunity to reduce their estate and shrink the tax bill their son—who will inherit everything anyway—will eventually have to pay.*

Both Joe and Faye take advantage of their $10,000 exemption to give a total of $20,000 to their son and another $20,000 to his wife. As soon as the first of the year rolls around, they can give away that much again if they're still feeling well-off and altruistic.

2. How Gifts Can Add Up

Using the annual exclusion repeatedly over a number of years can greatly reduce the size of your estate—and so, the ultimate estate tax bill. Let's say you give $7,000 each to your two children, three years in a row; none of this $42,000 is subject to gift tax. If you give $10,000 per year to one person for five years, you've given away $50,000 tax-free. If you gave the same $50,000 to the same person in one year, you would get only one $10,000 exemption; $40,000 would be subject to tax.

Example: *Patti owns a successful small business, with an estimated net worth of $2 million. Her other assets are worth roughly $475,000. Patti intends to leave her business to her four children. To reduce the value of her eventual estate, she incorporates her business and starts giving her children stock. She can give each of her children stock worth $10,000 per year gift tax-free—a yearly total of $40,000. For ten years, she gives each child $10,000 worth of stock, transferring a total of $400,000 tax-free.*

MAKING SURE A GIFT-GIVING PROGRAM KEEPS GIVING

If you plan to make a series of tax-free (or even taxable) gifts over many years, you should take one step to make sure that your plans aren't interrupted if you become incapacitated. That step is to sign a document called a Durable Power of Attorney for Finances.

In a durable power of attorney, you choose someone to handle your financial affairs if, someday, you can't. If you want this person (called your attorney-in-fact) to be able to keep making gifts of your property, you'll need to spell out that authority in the document.

For more information and forms, see *The Power of Attorney Handbook*, by Shae Irving (Nolo Press).

3. Timing Your Gifts

You can make the most of the $10,000 exemption if you keep in mind that it is based on a calendar year. If you miss a year, you can't go back and claim the exclusion. But if you spread a large gift over two or more years, you may escape gift tax complications.

Example: *If you give your daughter $20,000 on December 17, $10,000 of it is taxable. You'll have to file a gift tax return (by April 15 of the next year), and you'll use up $10,000 of the total amount you can give away or leave tax-free.*

But if you give her $10,000 in December, and wait a couple of weeks before handing over the other $10,000 on January 1, both gifts are tax-free. They don't reduce the estate tax credit available to your estate after your death.

Not only cash can be split. You can give some stocks now, some next year. You can even give real estate in pieces—physical pieces, if that's possible, or pieces (percentages) of ownership. (For a discussion of what kind of property makes a good gift—from a tax standpoint—see Section C, below.)

Example: *Solomon and his wife Rhoda want to give their vacation cabin to their son Gerard. The cabin has a fair market value of $75,000, but their equity is only $40,000; there is still $35,000 left to pay on the mortgage. In November, Solomon and Rhoda sign a deed transferring the cabin to Rhoda and Gerard as joint tenants. That means that Rhoda and Gerard each own a 1/2 interest in the property. Gerard's share is worth $20,000; the gift from his parents is tax-free because together, they can give him up to $20,000 tax-free each calendar year.*

The next calendar year, Rhoda gives her half-share, worth $20,000, to Gerard. Even though only Rhoda makes the gift, the IRS considers it, for tax purposes, to have come from both spouses.

⚠ **Special rules apply when you make tax-free gifts to children.** *Gifts to minors must be structured so they don't run afoul of IRS rules. See Section G, below.*

4. Gifts That Don't Qualify for the Exclusion

The annual gift tax exclusion applies only to gifts of what is called a "present interest." For the great majority of gifts, this is no problem.

If you must give the recipient the right to use the property immediately, you've given a present interest. By contrast, gifts that someone can use only in the future are called gifts of a "future interest," and they do not qualify for the annual exclusion

Example: *Kim gives $10,000 outright to her son Dale and places another $10,000 in an irrevocable trust for her daughter Madeleine. Madeleine, age 22, cannot use principal from the trust until she turns 35. The gift to Dale is a gift of a present interest, because he gets the money now. The gift to the trust for Madeleine is a gift of a future interest, because she has no right to the money now. Gift tax is assessed against the $10,000 Kim gives to the trust.*

Some other kinds of gifts are not eligible for the annual exclusion, either. See Sections F, Gifts to Trusts, and G, Gifts to Children, below.

⚠ *Ingenious taxpayers (and their lawyers) have come up with all sorts of ways to make the $10,000 exemption work overtime for them. But it's best not to get too fancy—certainly not without expert advice. Section E, below, discusses some schemes that don't work.*

C. What to Give—And What to Keep

Like everything else connected with gift-giving, the kind of property you choose to give away—for example, cash, stocks or real estate—can have tax consequences for you and for the recipient.

⚠️ **You can give only what's yours.** *If you and your spouse own property together, it's best to get your spouse's consent before you give it (or even your share) away. If your spouse doesn't want to join you in making the gift, you'll have to figure out exactly what you own. That can be difficult, especially in community property states (Arizona, California, Idaho, Louisiana, Nevada, New Mexico, Texas, Washington and Wisconsin). For help, see* Plan Your Estate, *by Denis Clifford and Cora Jordan (Nolo Press).*

1. Property That Is Likely to Increase in Value

If you're trying to decide what to give away, look among your assets for property that you expect will go up in value. If you hold onto it until your death, your estate will be worth that much more, and estate taxes will be correspondingly higher.

Giving this property away now not only excludes its present worth from your estate, but also eliminates the value of its future appreciation from your estate. For example, if you and your spouse give your son stock worth $20,000, you don't pay any gift tax. If the stock doubles in value over the next few years, you've actually removed $40,000 from your taxable estate.

Even making taxable gifts (and thus using up some of your personal estate tax exemption) may be an excellent approach to tax planning. That's because you don't have to actually pay any tax until you've given away or left property worth the whole exempt amount, $650,000 to $1 million. (Section H, below, discusses the advantages of making taxable gifts.)

Example: *Brooke, in her 60s, recently bought some undeveloped land for $160,000 cash. The property is located in an area she believes will be ripe for development in a few years. She intends to leave this land to her son, Lars, when she dies. If she waits to transfer the property until her death—probably at least 20 years away—then the market value of the land when she dies will be included in her taxable estate. It might be worth $800,000 by then. But if*

Brooke gives the land to Lars soon after buying it, none of its appreciation in value will be included in her taxable estate.

True, the gift will be subject to gift tax. The first $10,000 will be exempt, but $150,000 won't be, so the estate tax exemption available to Brooke's estate will be reduced by $150,000. Still, if the land does increase in value to $800,000, the gift tax assessed will be far less than the estate tax imposed on the appreciated property at Brooke's death.

Give a life insurance policy. *It's not exactly a traditional stocking-stuffer, but giving someone a life insurance policy you own can be a good way of reducing estate taxes. That's because if you own the policy at your death, its proceeds are included in your taxable estate. (Chapter 7 explains how it works.)*

2. Property That Has Increased in Value

It's often a poor idea, financially speaking, to give away property that has already gone up substantially in value since you acquired it. This is especially true if you are older and likely to die before too many years pass.

To understand why, you need to understand the concept of "tax basis." That's the amount from which taxable profit or loss is calculated when property is sold. Although this may sound like a tricky concept, it's actually pretty simple. Just keep in mind that a low basis means more taxable profit from a sale; a high basis means less taxable profit.

If you leave appreciated property at your death, the recipient's tax basis is the property's market value at your death. The basis is raised, or "stepped up," from your basis (usually, what you paid for it) to its current value.

By contrast, if you give that person the property while you're alive, the recipient's basis is just the same as yours. This, in tax jargon, is called the "carry-over" basis. Because the property has gone up in value, this basis is less than the current market value. In short, the recipient gets a lower basis than if he or she had inherited the property at the previous owner's death. That, in turn, means higher taxes down the line.

Example: *Years ago, Vinny paid $100,000 for a piece of land. His purchase price is his tax basis. The land's value has gone up to $500,000.*

If he gives the land to his niece, Jackie, her tax basis is $100,000, too. If she turns around and sells it for the current value, $500,000, she'll have to pay capital gains tax on her $400,000 gain.

If, instead, Jackie inherits the land from Vinny, her tax basis will be the market value of the property at the time of Vinny's death—not Vinny's $100,000 basis. If the value of the property is still $500,000 when Vinny dies, and Jackie sells the land for that amount, she'll have zero taxable gain.

TAX BASIS OF APPRECIATED PROPERTY

Transfer Method	Recipient's Basis	Result at Sale
Given during life	Same as giver's ("carry-over" basis)	Higher taxable profit
Left at death	Market value at time of death ("stepped-up" basis)	Lower taxable profit

This stepped-up basis rule can mean major capital gains tax savings for the recipient if an appreciated asset is transferred at death, not while the giver is still alive.

Example: *Bill bought 1,000 shares of stock at $5 per share. The shares are now worth $70 each and are still going up. If he gives the stock now to his daughter Betsy, her basis will be $5 per share. If he leaves it to Betsy at his death, her stepped-up basis in the stock will be the market price when he dies—probably $70 per share or higher, if the company continues to prosper.*

This difference will be vitally important when Betsy sells the stock. If her basis is $5 per share and she sells for $70 per share, she will have to pay capital gains tax on $65 per share, a total taxable profit of $65,000. By contrast, if her basis is stepped up to $70 because the transfer is made at death, and she sells the stock at $70 a share, she won't owe any capital gains tax.

Obviously, how the tax basis rules should affect your actions depends on your particular situation. If, for personal reasons, you want to make a gift of appreciated property now, and expect to live another 25 years, you won't want to postpone the transfer until your death just for some hypothetical, faraway tax savings. And now that the top long-term capital gains tax rate has been cut to 20%, it's one factor to consider— but certainly not the only one.

FIGURING YOUR TAX BASIS

When you buy property, your basis is generally the price you paid. In fact, basis is often referred to as cost basis. But if you make capital improvements—for example, adding a deck to your house—the cost of the improvement is added to your basis in the property. Maintenance and repair expenses, on the other hand, don't increase your basis.

Basis can also be adjusted down. For example, if you take depreciation deductions on your income tax return, the amount of the tax benefit is subtracted from your basis.

💡 **Different rules apply to charities.** *There's an important exception to the rule that it's often a bad idea to give away appreciated property: When you're giving to charities, it can be to your financial advantage to donate appreciated property. (See Chapter 6.)*

ONE SOLUTION FOR APPRECIATED STOCKS

Many elderly people who have lots of appreciated securities don't want to sell them because of the high capital gains tax that would result. On the other hand, they don't want to keep all those assets because they expect them to continue to go up in value, making the eventual estate tax bill higher.

One solution: Borrow against the securities, and give the borrowed cash to adult children or other family members. The loan can be paid back at death, when the assets are sold. This strategy gets the appreciation out of the older person's estate. And as long as the securities do increase in value, the interest paid on the loan will be more than made up for by estate and capital gains tax savings.

It's common to borrow up to one-third of the value of the securities. If you're interested in this idea, talk to your stockbroker.

D. Ways to Make Gifts

There are lots of ways to structure gifts—you don't just have to reach for your checkbook. Here are some options.

1. Make an Interest-Free Loan

If you loan someone money interest-free or at an artificially low interest rate, you're making a gift. You're giving the borrower the amount of the interest that you're not charging. According to the IRS, an "artificially low" interest rate is any rate below market interest rates when the loan was made. Each month, the IRS publishes a standard rate in its *Internal*

Revenue Bulletin; you can check there (it's available on the IRS Web site at www.irs.ustreas.gov) or contact an IRS office.

Such a gift, like any other, is potentially taxable. Because of the $10,000 annual gift tax exclusion, however, most interest-free loans don't have gift tax consequences. For example, at 10% annual simple interest, you can make an interest-free loan of $100,000 to someone without gift tax liability. A married couple could loan someone up to $200,000 interest-free before the annual interest would exceed $20,000, the couple's combined annual gift tax exclusion.

2. Create an Irrevocable Trust

Transferring property to an irrevocable trust—that is, one you can't change or end if you change your mind—is another way of making a gift. For example, you might transfer property to an irrevocable trust set up to benefit a permanently disabled adult.

By contrast, naming someone as a beneficiary in a will or revocable living trust document doesn't guarantee he or she will receive the property, so no gift is made. You could tear up the will tomorrow, and the (former) beneficiary would never get a thing.

Most irrevocable trusts are created as part of a will or living trust, and don't become operational until the grantor (the person who sets up the trust) dies. But there can be reasons to create an irrevocable trust that is operational as soon as you create it, while you're still alive.

For example, you might create an irrevocable trust just to own a life insurance policy. If you transfer the policy to the trust, it, not you, will be the policy's legal owner at your death. The current value of the policy will be a taxable gift, but making this gift removes the proceeds of the policy from your taxable estate. The result is that your estate will save more in estate tax than it will pay in gift tax (which usually isn't paid until your death anyway, remember). Either way, you can direct the proceeds of the policy to the same beneficiary. (See Chapter 7.)

Other types of irrevocable trusts include:

- A "special needs" trust for a disabled person who will need lifetime help managing money. A well-designed special needs trust won't reduce the beneficiary's eligibility for government assistance.

- A "Grantor-Retained Income Trust," which lets you transfer property now but retain the right to receive income from it. This is a sophisticated trust used by wealthy people to save on estate and gift taxes. You transfer property to the trust, then retain an interest in the property for a set period of years; after that time, the property goes to the trust beneficiaries.

More information about trusts. *All these varieties of trusts, and many others, are explained in* Plan Your Estate, *by Denis Clifford and Cora Jordan (Nolo Press). You'll need a knowledgeable attorney to prepare the actual trust documents.*

3. Forgive a Debt

If someone owes you money, and you forgive (cancel) the debt, you have made a gift in the amount of the debt. If you don't forgive more than $10,000 per person per year, gifts you make this way are not subject to gift tax.

Forgiving debts year after year, however, can get tricky. For example, if you loan someone (especially a family member) $100,000 and then forgive $10,000 every year, the IRS will probably conclude that you never intended the borrower to pay you back, and that you really were just giving away the whole amount of the original "loan." (See Section E, Gifts That Can Land You in Tax Trouble, below.)

4. Assign a Mortgage or Debt Owed to You

If someone owes you a debt, you can give away the right to collect that debt. For example, if you sell your house and extend credit to the buyer, you can give your son the right to receive the buyer's mortgage payments. It's called "assigning" the mortgage. As with other gifts, if the amount you're giving this way exceeds $10,000 per year per recipient, you must file a gift tax return.

5. Make Someone a Co-Owner

If you put property that you own by yourself into joint ownership with another person, you're giving a half-interest in that property to the new co-owner.

Example: *Saul, a widower, puts his $100,000 house into joint tenancy with his daughter. This removes half the value of the house from Saul's estate (and also makes it possible for the house to pass to his daughter without probate at his death). Because the half-interest in the house is worth considerably more than $10,000, Saul must file a gift tax return.*

There are several ways, legally, to structure a shared ownership. If you own something with someone else as joint tenants, each owner must own an equal share. So if there are two owners, each must own a half-interest. That may create a problem (as it would for Saul in the previous example) if you're trying to keep your gifts under $10,000 per year per recipient.

One way to get around this problem may be to use a different form of co-ownership, called tenancy in common. Because tenants in common can own different-sized shares, you can give small interests away each year.

Example: *Saul makes his daughter a tenant in common with him, as co-owners of the house. He gives her a 10% interest in the house every year. Because the* *value of the 10% interest doesn't exceed $10,000, each transaction is completely free of gift tax.*

There is a special rule for joint bank accounts. If you set up a joint tenancy bank account with someone else and make deposits, you're not making a gift. The gift is made—and a gift tax return possibly required—only when the other joint owner withdraws money that you deposited.

E. Gifts That Could Land You in Tax Trouble

It's the IRS's job to look for estate planning strategies that cross the line from clever to forbidden. Here are a few gift-giving strategies frowned on by the feds. Tread very cautiously in these areas to avoid stirring up a gift tax problem.

1. Loans That Are Really Gifts

Some parents have made large loans to their children, intending to forgive the repayments $10,000 at a time. Sometimes the parents transfer a house to the children, who sign a mortgage with payments of $10,000 per year. The IRS, skeptical of these arrangements to start with, has set out rules you must follow if you want to prove that they are bona fide loans, not gifts in disguise. The bottom line seems to be that if you are meticulous about your paperwork, this strategy can be successful.

The IRS starts with the presumption that a transfer between family members is a gift. You can get around that presumption by showing that you really expected repayment and intended to enforce the debt. In making that determination, the IRS pays attention to whether or not:

- The borrower signed a promissory note.
- You charged interest.
- There was security (collateral) for the debt.

- You demanded repayment.
- The borrower actually repaid some of the loan.
- There was a fixed date that the loan was due to be repaid.
- The borrower had the ability to repay.
- Your records or those of the recipient indicated that the transfer was a loan.
- The transaction was reported, for federal tax purposes, as a loan.

In the case that prompted this slew of factors, a woman had loaned $100,000 to each of her two sons. They signed promissory notes, and the loans were duly recorded in the books of the family's business, but there was no deadline for repayment. One of the sons made a $15,000 repayment. Their mother never demanded any payments, and each year she sent a letter to the sons, stating that she had forgiven (canceled) some of the debt.

The IRS ruled, and the federal Tax Court agreed, that the loans had actually been gifts. The mother ended up not only owing gift tax on the whole amount, but missing out on the years when she could have been (and thought she was) making tax-free $10,000 annual gifts. (*Elizabeth B. Miller*, Tax Court Memo 1996-3.)

Proceed with caution. *If you want to set up an elaborate scheme for forgiving debts, form is everything. Unless you're quite confident that you've mastered all the rules, see a lawyer who's experienced in setting up such deals so that they pass IRS scrutiny.*

2. Gifts That Are Really Loans

A gift is something you transfer freely and permanently, without receiving anything in return. If it isn't clear that you've really made a gift, the IRS may conclude that you still own the property, and include it in your taxable estate.

From the point of view of the IRS, the crucial element in determining whether or not a gift is made is the giver's intent, which can sometimes be murky. For example, say you obtain a valuable painting from Frank. Did Frank intend to give you that painting, or loan it to you? Or was he hoping to sell it to you?

If there is no clear written evidence that a gift has been made, the IRS won't know, when you transfer something for less than its market value, whether you intend to make a gift or you're just a poor businessperson. So, it does the only thing it can do: It looks at the "objective evidence." If the evidence doesn't show that a gift was made, the IRS will include the property in the deceased person's estate, subject to estate tax if the estate is large enough.

Example: *When Max buys a new car, he lets his niece Ashley drive the old one, but never officially transfers ownership to Ashley's name. When Max dies unexpectedly, Ashley contends that Max gave the car to her and intended her to have it. But in the absence of any hard evidence to that effect, the car is considered part of Max's estate.*

If your intent may not be obvious (now or in the future), it's best to make a paper trail. Write up, sign and date a short statement that explains your intent to make a gift. Put it with your will. It will be strong evidence that you meant to make a gift if the IRS ever audits your estate.

Example: *Sebastian gives his daughter several pieces of very valuable furniture that have been in the family for two centuries. To forestall family fights and possible IRS inquiry, he writes a letter to his daughter, stating that he is making a gift of the furniture to her now. (If the total value of the pieces exceeds $10,000, he'll also need to file a federal gift tax return—or spread the gift over two or more calendar years.)*

3. Gifts Made to One Person but Intended for Another

The IRS won't be fooled if you give property to one person, but it's obvious that the intended recipient is someone else. For example, the IRS went after the estate of one man who had given annual gifts of stock to his son, daughter-in-law and grandchildren, classifying each gift as exempt because of the $10,000-per-recipient rule. For 14 years, the daughter-in-law had faithfully transferred her stock to her husband on the same day she received it. The IRS ruled that the stock was really for the son, and that the gifts to him had exceeded the $10,000 annual ceiling. (*Estate of Joseph Cidulka*, Tax Court Memo 1996-149.)

4. Gifts With Strings Attached

If you want to give it, give it. Don't try to hang onto any control over what you've given away, or legally there is no gift. The IRS regularly disallows gifts when it concludes that the property never really left the control of the purported giver.

Example 1: *Matt puts $10,000 into a desk drawer for Nina. There's no legal gift until Nina removes the money.*

Example 2: *Carl deeds his house over to his son, Ishmael, but retains the right to receive rent from the property. The transaction is not a legal gift. When Carl dies, the house will still be part of his estate, which means it may be subject to estate tax.*

Phony gifts fall into this category, too. If you claim, just for tax purposes, to give someone something, but don't really let the purported recipient get his or her hands on it, the IRS will consider the property part of your estate at your death.

LOOKING DEEPER INTO GIFTS

For a fascinating discussion of the varied meanings of giving, read *The Gift: Imagination and the Erotic Life of Property*, by Lewis Hyde (Random House). The book brilliantly explores the spirit involved in giving and receiving a gift, from a Christmas present to creating a work of art, and how the giving spirit interacts with commercial culture.

F. Gifts to Trusts

Whether or not a transfer to a trust is actually a gift, for IRS purposes, depends on the amount of control you keep over the trust property.

Property you place in a revocable living trust (a trust that you can change or revoke at any time) isn't a gift. That's because you retain full control over the property; you can withdraw it from the trust or revoke the whole trust. The beneficiaries you name in the trust document will inherit the property after your death, but they have no current right to the trust property.

If you transfer property to an irrevocable trust and give up all control over it, the transfer is a gift. (It may not, however, qualify for the $10,000 gift tax exclusion; see Section B, above.) But if you establish an irrevocable trust and reserve the right to change who will benefit from it (even if you, yourself, are specifically excluded as a possible beneficiary), your transfer of property to the trust is not a gift.

Example: *Roger, a wealthy older man, puts money in an irrevocable trust for his grandniece Olivia, to be used for her eventual college costs. He appoints a trustee and gives him the authority to alter the purposes for which the trust money can be spent. Roger also retains the right to substitute a new trustee. Because Roger still has so much control over the trust property, there has been no gift for gift tax purposes.*

G. Gifts to Children

Children are the natural objects of their adult relatives' affection and generosity. But giving them valuable property before they are adults raises several important questions.

1. Who Will Manage the Property?

Minors (in most states, children under 18) are not permitted to manage valuable property by themselves; an adult must be responsible. The ceiling varies from state to state, but minors commonly can't own more than a few thousand dollars without adult control.

Fortunately, it's quite easy to choose an adult to manage the property. You can arrange it by setting up either:

- a simple child's trust, or
- a custodianship authorized by state law.

The second way is easier: Name an adult to serve as "custodian" of the money. Custodians are authorized under a law called the Uniform Transfers to Minors Act (UTMA) or the Uniform Gifts to Minors Act, one of which has been adopted by every state.

All you need to do is appoint the custodian, in writing, and give the property to that person instead of to the child directly. The custodian has the legal responsibility to manage and use the money for the benefit of the child. When the child reaches adulthood, he or she gets whatever's left. In most states, the law requires the custodian to turn over the property when the child reaches age 21; in a few states, the age is 18. And a few other states allow you to choose an age between 18 and 25 at which the custodianship will end.

Example: *Sam wants to give $10,000 to his young grandson Tyler. Sam names his daughter, Tyler's mother, as custodian of the money, and she opens a bank account in the name of "Suzanne Houston, as custodian for Tyler Houston under the Texas Uniform Transfers to Minors Act." She will manage the money for Tyler until he turns 21. If there's anything left then, Tyler will get it outright.*

You can name only one custodian for one child. So if you want to make gifts to three children, you must set up three separate custodianships. The same person can be the custodian for each child, but each child's money must be kept separate.

AGE AT WHICH AN UTMA CUSTODIANSHIP ENDS

Alabama	21	Missouri	21
Alaska	18 to 25*	Montana	21
Arizona	21	Nebraska	21
Arkansas	18 to 21*	Nevada	18 to 25*
California	18 to 25*	New Hampshire	21
Colorado	21	New Jersey	18 to 21*
Connecticut	21	New Mexico	21
Delaware	21	New York	21
District of Columbia	18	North Carolina	18 to 21*
Florida	21	North Dakota	21
Georgia	21	Ohio	21
Hawaii	21	Oklahoma	18 to 21*
Idaho	21	Oregon	21
Illinois	21	Pennsylvania	21
Indiana	21	Rhode Island	18
Iowa	21	South Dakota	18
Kansas	21	Tennessee	21
Kentucky	18	Texas	21
Louisiana	18	Utah	21
Maine	18 to 21*	Virginia	18 to 21*
Maryland	21	Washington	21
Massachusetts	21	West Virginia	21
Minnesota	21	Wisconsin	21
Mississippi	21	Wyoming	21

*The person who sets up the custodianship can designate the age, within these limits, at which the custodianship ends and the beneficiary inherits the money outright.

IF YOUR STATE IS AN UTMA HOLDOUT

Only three states—Michigan, South Carolina and Vermont—still spurn the Uniform Transfers to Minors Act. These states do, however, have an older law, called the Uniform *Gifts* to Minors Act, on the books. It lets you name a custodian only for gifts made during your life, and provides that the custodianship must end when the minor turns 21. The Act also limits the kinds of property that can be given; only money, securities, life insurance policies and annuity contracts are permitted.

If you don't want to set up a custodianship, you can set up a child's trust instead. The trust document must set out the powers of the trustee and state when the trust property should be turned over to the beneficiary. If you create a trust, keep in mind that the transfer may not be a gift, for gift tax purposes. (See Section F, Gifts to Trusts, above.) The transfer must also meet special rules, discussed next, in order to qualify for the annual gift tax exclusion.

2. Special Gift Tax Rules

You must be careful if you want to give a tax-free gift to a young beneficiary. It's fine to set up a trust or custodianship (discussed just above) to handle the property for the minor. (Rev. Rul. 59-357, 1959-2.) But to qualify for the $10,000 annual exclusion, the gift must satisfy these conditions:

- The recipient must receive the property outright by age 21. This means that if you create a trust for the recipient, the trust document must state that the property will be turned over to the recipient by his or her 21st birthday. (You may, however, give the recipient the right to extend the trust for a longer period.) Similarly, if you set up a custodianship, it must end when the recipient turns 21. Some states allow a custodianship to last until the beneficiary is older than 21; don't choose this option if you're concerned about qualifying for the annual gift tax exclusion.

- The property and its income may be spent by, or for the benefit of, a recipient who isn't 21 yet. You can give the trustee or custodian wide latitude when it comes to spending trust income or property, but you can't limit his or her discretion too strictly.
- If the recipient dies before age 21, the remaining property must go to the recipient's estate or to someone the recipient named— for example, in a will.
- If you give the money to a trust, the trust must be irrevocable. This isn't a special rule for minors; it applies to all gifts made to a trust. (See Section F, above.) (26 U.S.C. § 2503(c).)

Example 1: *Biff decides to give an expensive thoroughbred horse worth $30,000 to his niece Brenda, age 16, who has loved horses since she was small. Biff makes the gift under his state's UTMA, which requires the horse to be legally turned over to Brenda when she becomes 21—which is fine with Biff. Biff names Brenda's mother, Josette, as custodian for the gift. They all know this is only technical, since Brenda will be, and wants to be, responsible for the horse.*

The first $10,000 of Biff's gift is free of gift tax. He is assessed gift tax on the remaining $20,000.

Example 2: *Oksana wants to be certain that her grandchildren Victor, 12, and Marya, 10, will have enough money to attend college. Oksana wants to make the gift now, so that her grandchildren will know their educational future is secure.*

To qualify for the $10,000 annual gift tax exclusion, the money must be turned over to the kids when they reach 21. Oksana doubts that any 21-year-old can responsibly handle large amounts of money—but she figures that given the cost of college, there won't be much left to give the kids by the time they're 21. So she names their father as custodian for a $10,000 gift to each child.

She transfers some more money to a trust for each grandchild, to last until the grandchild is 30. She names their father as trustee. Oksana realizes that by doing this, she will not obtain the annual gift tax exclusion for any money she gives the trust, because neither child will receive the money outright by age 21. But her concern about giving a 21-year-old a big bundle of money overrides any consideration of tax savings.

(If Oksana were in good health and her grandchildren were a little older, she might just decide to wait until they enter college, and make tax-free payments of their tuition. See Chapter 2.)

3. Income and Capital Gains Tax Considerations

If you give a child property that produces investment income—interest, dividends or capital gains—chances are he or she will pay less tax on the income than you would have. It all depends, however, on the age of the child.

- Children under 14 pay tax at their parents' highest income tax rate on all investment income of more than $1,300/year. (26 U.S.C. § 1(g).)

- Children 14 and over pay the same tax rates as do adults, and are unaffected by their parents' tax rate. So most of them, with relatively little income, are in the lowest tax brackets. Currently, an unmarried individual can earn a few thousand dollars without owing tax; the next bracket is 15%. Long-term capital gains are taxed at 10%.

These rules mean that giving valuable property to a young child—not yet 14—won't net you much of a tax break. But giving appreciated property to a child who is at least 14 years old can mean a substantial overall tax break for your family.

Example: *Realizing that his 15-year-old granddaughter Vanessa will soon need money for college, William gives her stock that has gone up in value, since he bought it, from $10/share to $40/share. Vanessa's earned income from a part-time job is less than $2,000 a year, so she is in the lowest tax brackets for income and capital gains tax. If she sells the stock while its price is still $40/share, she'll owe only 10% of the profit in tax; her grandfather would have to pay 20%.*

⚠ Be cautious when giving appreciated property. *Normally, appreciated property does not make a good gift from a tax standpoint. That's because the recipient gets your (low) tax basis in the property, and as a result has a lot of taxable profit if he or she sells the property. (See Section C.2, above.)*

H. Making Taxable Gifts

Although most of this chapter is devoted to explaining tax-free gifts, sometimes it can be to your family's financial advantage to make taxable gifts. This strategy can save many affluent families tens of thousands of dollars in estate tax.

Once you've used up your whole estate tax exemption ($650,000 to $1 million, depending on the year) by making taxable gifts, you'll have to pay gift tax when you make a taxable gift. Actually, you'll pay it the next year; gift tax returns are due at the same time as personal income tax returns. (Remember, you cannot choose to pay gift tax until you've used up your entire estate tax exemption; see the introductory chapter.)

The reason it can be good to pay that gift tax now is that if you pay it while you're alive, that money goes out of your estate; it won't be taxed at your death. But if the tax is paid after your death, it must be paid from estate funds—which are themselves subject to estate tax. An example should help make this somewhat confusing concept easier to grasp.

Example: *Lina, an elderly widower, has already used up her entire estate tax exemption by making taxable gifts. Now she is trying to decide whether to leave her $3 million estate to her son Zack at her death, or to give him a big chunk of it now.*

If Lina gives Zack $1 million now, and pays the gift tax due from the rest of her property, Zack will get $77,000 more than if Lina left everything to him at her death. Here's how the figures work out:

	Entire $3 million left at death	*$1 million given away during life, $2 million left at death*
Gift tax due	-0-	$144,000
Size of estate	$3 million	$1.856 million
Estate tax due at death	($1.089 million)	($868,000)
Amount Zack gets	$1.911 million	$1.988 million (gift + estate)

There is one very important exception to this rule. To discourage people from using this powerful tax-saving practice just before death, the IRS includes gift tax paid during the last three years of life in the taxable estate. (IRC § 2503.) In other words, if you are willing to part with your money at least three years before you die, the IRS treats your gift as a done deal. But if you wait too long, what you gave away is counted as part of your estate.

Example: *Lina gives her son $1 million and dies two years later. When Lina's executor calculates how much estate tax is owed, the amount of the gift tax Lina paid two years before her death must be added back into the gross estate, for tax purposes.*

JANUARY IS THE MOST GENEROUS MONTH

If you're the rare individual who has already made so many taxable gifts that you've used up your entire estate tax credit, the timing of your gifts can be important. Make taxable gifts near the beginning of the tax year, so that you do not have to pay the gift tax until April of the following year. In the meantime, the income from the gift will go to the recipient rather than increasing your taxable estate.

CHAPTER 2

Pay Tuition or Medical Expenses

Money spent directly for someone's medical bills or school tuition is not subject to federal gift/estate tax, no matter what the amount. (IRC § 2503(e)(2).) This exemption is in addition to the $10,000 annual gift tax exclusion discussed in Chapter 1. Using it can provide a great way to give loved ones help they really need and simultaneously reduce the size of your taxable estate.

You can make a tax-exempt gift for anyone's tuition—nursery school through graduate school—or medical expenses. The recipient doesn't have to be a relative.

A. How Payments Must Be Made

To qualify for this tax exemption, the money must be paid directly to the provider of the medical service or the school. (Treas. Reg. § 25.2503-6.) If you give money to an ill person or student who then pays the bills, your gift is not tax-exempt.

Example: *Horace gives his niece $14,000 so she can pay for unexpected medical bills that weren't covered by insurance. She deposits his check and writes three of her own the same day, to pay her doctors and the hospital. Horace's gift is not tax-exempt. The $4,000 that exceeds the $10,000 annual exclusion is subject to gift tax.*

Similarly, if you give money to a trust, providing that it is to be used to pay for your grandchildren's tuition, the gift is not tax-free. The trust, not the educational institution, is the recipient. The same goes for tuition pre-payment plans or savings accounts—they don't qualify as tax-free gifts.

Nor can you reimburse someone who has already paid a medical or tuition bill and have this be a tax-exempt gift.

Example: *Lisette gives her nephew Charles $12,000 to reimburse him for medical expenses he incurred while studying abroad. Under the annual gift* *tax exclusion, $10,000 of the gift is tax-free; the remaining $2,000 is a taxable gift. If Lisette had paid the medical bills directly, her entire gift would have been tax-free.*

B. Medical Expenses

If you pay someone's medical bills, or their health insurance premiums, your payments are not subject to gift tax. The payments must, as mentioned above, be made directly to anyone who provides medical care. If not, they are not are tax-exempt.

Payments for medical care include money spent for:

- Diagnosis, cure, mitigation, treatment or prevention of disease, or for the purpose of affecting any structure or function of the body.
- Transportation primarily for and essential to this medical care.
- Insurance that covers medical care.
- Lodging ("not lavish or extravagant under the circumstances") up to $50/night per person while away from home. Staying in the lodgings must be primarily for and essential to getting the medical care, and the care must be provided by a physician in a hospital or equivalent facility. Finally, there must be no "significant element" of personal pleasure or recreation in the travel. (IRC § 213(d).)

Cosmetic surgery and similar procedures aren't covered, unless they are necessary because of a disfiguring illness or injury.

Again, you cannot pay these expenses indirectly and claim the tax exemption.

You can get stung, from a tax standpoint, if you pay for medical care and insurance later reimburses the recipient. In that case, your gift no longer qualifies for the exclusion, to the extent of the reimbursement. IRS regulations say that you made the gift on the date the recipient received the reimbursement—even if you had no way of knowing that the expenses would be reimbursed.

Example: *Mathilda pays medical bills that total $21,000 for her adult son. Later, her son's insurance company changes its corporate mind and reimburses him for $18,000 of the expenses. Legally, Mathilda has made a gift of $18,000 to her son, as of the date he received the insurance company's reimbursement check. The first $10,000 of that amount is not subject to gift tax, because of the annual exclusion. The other $8,000 is subject to gift tax, and Mathilda will have to file a gift tax return.*

C. Tuition

Under IRS rules, only payments for tuition are tax-exempt. Tuition is what a school charges for education or training. If you pay for a student's other expenses, such as books, supplies or room and board, your generosity is not rewarded with a gift tax exclusion.

The tuition tax break applies to any level of schooling. For example, if you have several grandchildren who live where public grade schools are poor, footing the bill for their private school tuition could let you take many thousands out of your estate each year, and give you the satisfaction of making it possible for them to get a better education.

When it comes to higher learing, you're not limited just to traditional academic institutions such as colleges and universities. The law specifically applies to tuition for "education or training." Payments can be to any educational organization with a regular faculty and curriculum and a student body that regularly attends at a certain place. The educational organization doesn't even have to be in this country, as long as it meets the basic requirements. (IRC § 170(b)(1)(A)(ii).) The definition seems to include just about every kind of school except correspondence schools and mail-order diploma mills.

A student whose tuition you are underwriting can be enrolled part-time or full-time. (Treas. Reg. § 25.2503-6.)

CHAPTER 3

Leave or Give Property to Your Spouse

Ohne simple strategy for avoiding estate taxes is to leave your property to your spouse. If your spouse is a United States citizen, you can leave him or her a dime or a billion dollars, and none of it will be subject to estate tax.

If it sounds too good to be true, sometimes it can be. Especially late in life, leaving a large amount of property to your spouse probably won't avoid estate taxes; it will only postpone them until your spouse's death. As discussed below, the advisability of leaving a lot of property to your spouse depends on the size of your estate, your age and your health. First, though, let's look at the basic rules.

A. Spouses Who Are U.S. Citizens

The blanket exemption from federal estate tax for property inherited by a spouse is called the "marital deduction." (IRC § 2523(a).) The deduction is unlimited. And it doesn't make any difference how you own the property—for example, whether the property is owned entirely by one spouse, or by both in a form such as joint tenancy or community property. It all qualifies for the exemption.

No matter how much you leave tax-free to your spouse, your estate is still entitled to all other estate tax exemptions, including the personal estate tax exemption ($650,000 to $1 million, depending on the year of death).

Example 1: *When Judith dies in the year 2003, she leaves her share of the family house, worth $300,000, to her husband Bruno. She also leaves him other belongings worth a total of $100,000. Judith leaves $50,000 to her favorite charity. Finally, she leaves a sizable stock account, worth $400,000, to her children from a previous marriage.*

The personal estate tax exemption in 2003 is $700,000; Judith's estate totals $850,000. But no estate tax is owed. Everything left to Bruno is tax-free, and the charity's money is tax-free because of the charitable deduction. (See Chapter 6.) The $700,000 personal exemption more than covers the $400,000 left to the children.

Example 2: *Horace dies in 2006, leaving an estate worth $3 million. Half of that goes to his wife, Rebecca, outright. The rest goes to other beneficiaries.*

The $1.5 million left to Rebecca passes free of tax. Of the rest, $1 million is not taxed because in 2006, the personal estate tax exemption is $1 million. The remaining $500,000 is subject to tax.

B. Non-Citizen Spouses

If your spouse is not a U.S. citizen, property he or she inherits from you is **not** eligible for the marital deduction. This is true even if the spouse is a legal resident of this country. The reason for the rule, apparently, is that Congress was afraid non-citizens would inherit lots of money from their citizen-spouses, and then pick up and take it out of the country, where the IRS could never get another crack at it.

You can, however, use all or part of your personal estate tax exemption for property you leave your spouse. That can shelter a substantial amount from tax.

Example 1: *Simone is married to Jason, a non-U.S. citizen. She dies in 2002 with an estate of $630,000. She leaves $500,000 to Jason, and the rest to their children. None of this is covered by the marital deduction. But because her total estate is under the estate tax threshold for 2002, $700,000, no estate tax is due.*

Example 2: *Bill's wife Tara is not a U.S. citizen. Bill dies in 2007, leaving his entire $1.5 million estate to her. Because the marital deduction does not apply, only the amount of the personal estate tax exemption for that year, $1 million, is excluded from tax. His estate will owe tax on the remaining $500,000.*

If you want to leave your non-citizen spouse a big chunk of money, and this law promises to mess up your plans, there are a couple of things you can do:

- Give money to your non-citizen spouse while you're alive. You can give property worth up to $100,000 tax-free each year. (Treas. Reg. § 2523(i)(2).)

Example: *If Bill, in the previous example, had given Tara $100,000 a year in the five years before he died, his estate would have been cut down to $1 million and would not have owed any estate tax.*

- Ask your spouse to apply for citizenship. If your spouse is a permanent resident of this country but just never saw a reason to become a U.S. citizen, here's the reason. (You might want to reassure your spouse that it is no longer necessary to renounce the citizenship of another nation when acquiring U.S. citizenship.)
- Use a Qualified Domestic Trust (QDOT) to defer estate taxes that would otherwise be due at your death. QDOTs are discussed in detail in Chapter 5.

C. When Using the Marital Deduction Makes Sense— and When It Doesn't

Leaving your spouse an unlimited amount of money free of federal estate tax is not, for many older people, the answer to their estate tax worries. Although it eliminates estate tax on the first death, a problem can crop up when the *second* spouse dies. A widow or widower who has inherited a lot of money may have a very large estate—and when he or she dies, there's no marital deduction to wipe out the estate tax bill.

For example, say you and your spouse have a combined estate, owned equally, of $1.8 million. If you die first, in 2006, and leave everything to your spouse, she will wind up with $1.8 million. If she dies in 2009, when the estate tax exemption is $1 million, $800,000 will be subject to estate tax (the $1.8 million minus the $1 million exemption). The tax bill: $345,000.

In contrast, if each of you had used your personal estate tax exemption when you left the property, none of it would have been subject to tax. Both your share and your spouse's would have been under the estate tax threshold.

The same principle applies to even larger estates.

Example: *Gil and Kelly have an estate of $4 million, owned equally. Gil dies in 2006, leaving his $2 million to Kelly. No tax is due. Kelly, whose estate is now $4 million, dies later the same year. Of her estate, $1 million is exempt under the personal exemption, and $3 million is subject to tax.*

If Gil had left no property to Kelly, $1 million of his $2 million estate would have been taxed. The same would be true of Kelly's $2 million estate. So a total of only $2 million would have been subject to tax. And each million would have been taxed separately, at a lower rate than applies to the $3 million Kelly leaves.

In a nutshell, if both spouses are older, leaving property outright from one to the other usually either creates a taxable estate where there didn't have to be one, or greatly increases the tax on the surviving spouse's estate. (The best way to leave property for the use of a surviving spouse and still minimize overall estate tax is to use a bypass (AB) trust; see Chapter 4.)

Relying on the marital deduction to avoid estate tax makes sense only if one of you is young enough to expect to survive for a good number of years after the other spouse dies. Given that in a large number of marriages one spouse is at least 10 years younger than the other, and considering that on average women outlive men by about five years, this is very commonly true.

Leaving property directly to your spouse certainly offers the advantage of simplicity. No trusts, no paperwork—the survivor gets it outright. Assuming the surviving spouse lives for more than a few years, he or she has plenty of time to avoid eventual estate tax by spending some of the money or making tax-free gifts (using the $10,000 annual gift tax exclusion discussed in Chapter 1).

When are you too old to comfortably rely on the marital deduction? There are no fixed rules. It depends on your health, your desire to do (or put off) estate tax planning and your chronological age. As a very rough rule, age 65 or 70 seems to be the common dividing line.

Here are some quick generalizations that may help you decide.

You're both young. If your statistical chances of dying are still small, you and your spouse should consider holding off on fancy estate planning and just leave your property to each other. If the unexpected does happen, and one of you dies young, the survivor will probably have many years to spend the money he or she inherits, reducing the suddenly enlarged estate. Again, there's no magic age at which tax planning suddenly becomes imperative. It depends on how comfortable you feel with waiting, and how much time, money and energy you want to expend on estate planning.

Example: *Hal and Sumi, both in their late 50s, have a shared estate of $1.1 million. If one dies now and leaves everything to the other, the survivor will have an estate that's over the estate tax threshold. Still, they decide that for now, leaving all property to the other is their best plan.*

Their reasons: First, they have three college-aged children. Over the next few years, the costs of college (and maybe graduate school) will eat up a large part of their money, and bring it well under the estate tax threshold. Second, they expect to live many, many more years. Estate tax concerns can wait.

One of you is young. If one spouse is considerably younger than the other, the older spouse may want to make use of the marital deduction to avoid estate tax. Again, the rationale is that the younger spouse will be the survivor, and will have plenty of time to either spend the inherited money or come up with some other way to reduce estate tax at his or her death.

Example: *Lisette, age 71, marries Joe, age 62. Lisette's estate is worth $850,000. Joe's is worth $400,000. Lisette decides to leave all her property outright to Joe. Assuming she dies before he does, which is statistically likely, she wants him to continue to live in the comfortable style they both love. She's not worried that Joe's estate may wind up owing estate tax. She has no children she's trying to preserve any of her property for. Realistically, Joe would probably spend enough of the money to bring his estate below the estate tax threshold by the time he dies. And if he doesn't, "c'était la vie."*

You have children from a previous marriage. If you're in your second (or subsequent) marriage, providing for family members fairly is probably a greater concern than are eventual estate taxes. Instead of leaving lots of money to each other, you may want to keep your assets separate, perhaps with the help of a prenuptial agreement, and transfer much of your property directly (by gift or at your death) to your children.

How to talk to family members about touchy subjects. *For practical advice on how older couples can deal with these kinds of family concerns openly and fairly, see* Get a Life: You Don't Need a Million to Retire Well, *by Ralph Warner (Nolo Press).*

D. Combining the Marital Deduction With Other Tax-Saving Methods

A common estate tax plan is to make use of the marital deduction for some, but not all, of a spouse's estate. The idea is to maximize the use of all available estate tax exemptions.

Example: *Patricia and Raphael have assets of $3 million, owned equally. Each adopts the following estate plan for his $1.5 million share:*

- *$600,000 will be left outright to their adult child. This is tax-free under the personal estate tax exemption.*
- *$100,000 will be left to tax-exempt charities.*
- *The rest will be left outright to the surviving spouse.*

The tax result: an estate tax bill of zero.

Combining the marital deduction with the personal estate tax exemption is discussed further in Chapter 4.

E. Making Gifts to Your Spouse to Equalize Your Estates

Estate tax rates start off high—currently, 37%—and grow even higher as the size of the estate grows. So if one member of a couple has a much larger estate than the other does, they can pay less total tax if they shift some of the wealthier person's property over to the other spouse. The result is two smaller estates, each taxed at a lower rate (or not at all), instead of one large estate taxed at a higher rate.

Example: *Ned and Hannah have a combined estate of $1.2 million. Ned, who is 15 years older than Hannah, owns $800,000 of that amount. If he gives $200,000 to Hannah, their estates will each be worth $600,000—under the estate tax threshold.*

CHAPTER 4

Use a Bypass (AB) Trust

A "bypass" trust is a popular way to lessen or eliminate overall estate taxes. Both couples and individuals can use bypass trusts, but the most popular form of this trust, commonly called an "AB" trust, is used only by couples. In fact, it is a standard component of most estate plans lawyers prepare for affluent older couples, married or not. The AB trust sometimes goes by other names, such as a "credit shelter trust," an "exemption trust" or a "marital life estate trust."

TRUST BASICS

A trust, like a corporation, is an entity that exists only on paper but is legally capable of owning property. You can create a trust by preparing and signing a document called a Declaration (or Instrument) of Trust. Once the trust has been created, you can transfer property to it. If you name yourself as "trustee," however, you keep control over the trust assets. People commonly name themselves as trustee for trusts they set up during their lives.

The most common kind of trust is a basic probate-avoidance trust. You set up this kind of trust while you're alive, and transfer some or all of your assets to it. While you're alive, you control the trust and can revoke it at any time. In the trust document, you state who you want to inherit the trust property after your death. The "successor trustee," the person you name to take over the trust after your death, will distribute the trust property to the beneficiaries you named, without the need for probate court proceedings.

A. The Estate Tax Trap for Married Couples

You may wonder why a married couple would need a tax-saving trust. After all, one spouse can leave the other an unlimited amount of money absolutely free of federal estate tax, because of the marital deduction. (See Chapter 3.) The answer lies in what happens when the *second* spouse dies. For couples with a combined estate exceeding the estate tax threshold, a tax trap awaits. That's because the surviving spouse typically ends up with double the property, but only the same personal exemption from estate tax.

THE FEDERAL ESTATE TAX THRESHOLD

Year of Death	No Estate Tax If Taxable Estate Less Than:
1999	$650,000
2000-2001	$675,000
2002-2003	$700,000
2004	$850,000
2005	$950,000
2006 and after	$1 million

For example, take a couple with combined assets, owned equally, of $1.4 million. If the first spouse to die leaves everything to the other, the survivor will wind up with the whole $1.4 million. An estate that size will owe estate tax, even given the coming increases in the estate tax threshold. Say the first spouse dies in 2000 and the second in 2007, when the estate tax exemption is $1 million. When the second spouse dies, $400,000 will be subject to estate tax (the $1.4 million minus the $1 million exemption). The tax is a whopping $167,000.

This tax trap is particularly dangerous when both spouses are elderly. The survivor isn't likely to live long enough to really benefit from legally owning the deceased spouse's property, or to reduce the estate by making tax-free gifts. (See Chapter 1.)

With an AB trust, this tax trap can be eliminated. Here's how.

First, you sign a document that creates the AB trust, but provides that it won't become operational until your death. You name your spouse as the "life beneficiary" of this trust, and your children (or other persons) as the "final beneficiaries." If you die first, your trust property is left for your spouse's benefit, with certain restrictions required by law and any other restrictions you impose. Normally, the surviving spouse receives income generated by the trust property, and may even spend the trust property (principal) itself for basic needs such as medical care. When your spouse dies, your children inherit, outright, everything that's left in the trust.

The key to the tax savings is that your spouse never becomes the legal owner of the trust property. In other words, it bypasses his or her estate. And because it is not part of your spouse's estate, it is **not** subject to estate tax when he or she dies. It is subject to estate tax only at your death. If its value is under the estate tax threshold, no estate tax is due.

By contrast, if you leave your property to your spouse outright, it will be included as part of her taxable estate when she dies.

Example: *Arnold and Maggie share ownership of $1.6 million worth of property. They have three adult children. Maggie and Arnold both die after 2006, when the personal estate tax exemption will be $1 million. Maggie dies first, and Arnold a year later. Take a look at the difference that creating an AB trust can make:*

At Maggie's Death:	WITHOUT AN AB TRUST (everything left to Arnold)	WITH AN AB TRUST (everything left in trust for Arnold for life, then to children)
Value of estate	$800,000	$800,000
Marital deduction	($800,000)	($0)
Personal exemption	($0)	($1 million)
Tax due on	=$0	=$0
Estate tax due	$0	$0

At Arnold's Death:		
Value of estate	$1.6 million (his $800,000 plus $800,000 from Maggie)	$800,000 (because trust property not counted)
Personal exemption	($1 million)	($1 million)
Tax due on	=$600,000	=$0
Estate tax due	$255,800	$0

Neat, isn't it? By using an AB trust, no estate tax is paid. By contrast, without the trust, $255,800 must be handed over to the IRS, instead of to the children.

B. AB Trust Basics

The rest of this chapter goes into the details of AB trusts. But first, here's a bare-bones look at the process. The alphabet soup may seem confusing at first, but remember that the main point of it all is simple: Your property goes first to your spouse (with some limits to keep the IRS happy), and then to your kids (or other beneficiaries you choose).

The trust document. Usually, AB trust provisions are combined with a basic living trust, which is set up to avoid probate. That way, with one document, you can both avoid probate and eliminate estate tax.

Trust property. Normally, each spouse puts the bulk, or all, of his or her property into the AB trust. You can place in the trust whatever property you want—your separate property, your half of shared property or any portion of either. Leave the rest of your property directly to your kids, charities or other beneficiaries.

The A and the B. The trust document directs that when the first spouse dies, the AB trust must be split into two separate trusts: Trust A for property of the first spouse to die, and Trust B for the property of the surviving spouse. You and your spouse each name the other as the life beneficiary of your Trust A. You each also name final beneficiaries—typically, your children—for your Trust A. (Splitting trust assets between Trust A and Trust B can be a complicated undertaking. See Section C.3, below.)

When one spouse dies. Only one spouse's Trust A ever becomes operational: the Trust A of the first spouse to die. (The surviving spouse's Trust A cannot become operational because its life beneficiary, the other spouse, is already deceased.) The surviving spouse continues to have a separate revocable living trust, Trust B. It's completely under her control. She can leave that trust as it is, spend the money in it or amend it as she sees fit—for example, she can add or delete property or change beneficiaries.

Surviving spouses' rights. The surviving spouse receives a "life interest" in the other spouse's property (in Trust A). You can impose any restrictions you want over your spouse's rights to Trust A property, but both spouses commonly give the other the maximum permitted rights. These are the rights to:

- receive all trust income, and
- spend trust principal for the surviving spouse's "health, education, support and maintenance in his or her accustomed manner of living." (Treas. Reg § 20.2041-1(c)(2).)

To make sure all this really happens, the surviving spouse is, in most cases, named the trustee (as well as the beneficiary) of Trust A. That puts the surviving spouse in charge of trust assets and lets her spend trust money for any allowed purpose. Most trustees have the right to determine how Trust A property is used—for example, who can live in a house the trust owns. Trustees also manage trust assets; a trustee might, for example, sell an investment that's going downhill and invest the proceeds in something more promising. (Trustees' rights and duties are discussed in Section E, below.)

When the second spouse dies. When the surviving spouse dies, her final beneficiaries inherit the Trust B property. The surviving spouse has no power, however, to decide who receives any Trust A property left at her or his death. That decision was made by the deceased spouse, when the original trust document was written.

The estate tax break. Now, we get to the reason affluent couples establish these trusts in the first place. Because Trust A property never belongs to the surviving spouse, it is subject to tax only once, when the first spouse dies. If Trust A assets increase in value by the time the second spouse dies, this appreciation is not subject to estate tax.

Example: *Isabel and Simon own shared assets totaling $1.4 million. They each draft an AB trust for their $700,000, with their children as the final beneficiaries. Isabel dies in 2002, when the estate tax exemption is $700,000, so no tax is due on her Trust A property.*

Simon lives for another 20 years without spending any of the Trust A principal. At Simon's death, the Trust A property is worth $1.5 million. No estate tax is assessed against the Trust A property when Simon dies. The full $1.5 million is now distributed to the final beneficiaries free of estate tax.

C. Is an AB Trust for You?

AB trusts work very well for many families, but they aren't for everyone. Before deciding to use an AB trust, you and your spouse should understand what you're getting into. Once one spouse dies, that spouse's Trust A becomes irrevocable; it imposes limits and burdens on the survivor that cannot be changed. There are other important considerations as well.

1. Your Age

Commonly, it's only as a couple reaches their 50s or 60s that they consider creating an AB trust. Younger couples, unless they are quite wealthy, usually don't want to risk tying up $650,000 to $1 million of a deceased spouse's assets in an irrevocable Trust A. If one spouse dies prematurely, the surviving spouse might well live for decades. In that case, he or she would probably be better off inheriting the deceased spouse's property outright. As mentioned above, the survivor would inherit everything estate tax-free, no matter what the amount. That surviving spouse would probably have many years to use the money— and to arrange other methods of reducing any eventual estate tax bill.

Similarly, if one spouse is considerably younger than the other and presumably will live much longer, you may not want an AB trust. Generally there's no need to burden the younger spouse with a trust designed to save estate tax when he or she is likely to live for many years.

2. Your Intended Beneficiaries

An AB trust works well only if you want to leave all, or at least the bulk, of your property for the use of your surviving spouse. If, instead, you plan to leave substantial amounts of property directly to other beneficiaries (perhaps because your spouse already has plenty of money), an AB trust isn't necessary.

3. Legal Fees

Many people prepare good, legally valid AB trust documents without a lawyer. But when the first spouse dies, the survivor may well have to pay a lawyer or tax accountant for some help. Splitting the couple's assets into Trust A and Trust B at the first spouse's death, in a way that yields the greatest tax benefits, can be a tricky job.

a. Setting Up the Trust

Some couples—though certainly not all—feel perfectly comfortable preparing an AB trust themselves, without hiring an attorney. Trust language is fairly standard and easily available. If you and your spouse have a combined estate worth between $650,000 and $2 million, quite possibly you can go it alone. You can find forms and complete instructions for preparing an AB trust in *Make Your Own Living Trust,* by Denis Clifford (Nolo Press). The AB trust in that book is designed for couples who want to allow the surviving spouse the maximum legal rights the IRS allows over the Trust A property, while still gaining the estate tax-saving advantages of an AB trust. (See Section D, below.)

You'll definitely need to see a lawyer if:

- You and your spouse expect to have a combined estate exceeding twice the estate tax threshold. A good estate planning lawyer can help you explore more sophisticated options for reducing estate tax.
- You want to limit the rights of the surviving spouse to use Trust A property. This includes many couples with children from prior marriages, who want to be sure the bulk of their property is preserved for those children.

If you go to a lawyer, you'll probably pay several thousand dollars for an AB trust. Some lawyers charge an hourly rate for this work; experienced estate planning attorneys command $200 or more per hour. Others charge a flat fee, commonly in the $5,000 range.

CHILDREN FROM PREVIOUS MARRIAGES

If you have children from a previous marriage, you may want to name them as your final beneficiaries, while your spouse names someone else. That's no problem with an AB trust. You and your spouse each create your own separate AB trust, so each of you has the right to choose the final beneficiaries for your own trust property.

---

b. Dividing Property When One Spouse Dies

When the first spouse dies, the couple's shared property must be divided into two legally separate entities, Trust A and Trust B. That takes some work. Trust A, remember, contains the deceased spouse's property, which the surviving spouse can benefit from but does not legally own. Trust B, a revocable trust, contains the surviving spouse's own property and is under his complete control.

To best divide the couple's assets between Trust A and Trust B, an estate lawyer or accountant will probably be needed. Each item of the couple's shared property does not have to be divided 50-50 between the two trusts, but the total value of shared property in each trust must be equal. Although this flexibility is welcome, it often takes an expert to decide on the best division of assets between the two trusts. Different allocations may have very different tax consequences.

For example, what should be done with the family home? Let's say you allocate full ownership of the house to Trust B, the survivor's revocable trust. If the surviving spouse lives for many more years, the house would probably be worth considerably more (given inflation) by the date of his death. Its increased value might raise the value of the survivor's estate to a point where estate tax is due. Or, if his estate were already large enough to owe taxes, it would increase the tax bill.

If you include the full value of the home in Trust A, any increase in its value will not be subject to estate tax. But certain other tax advantages are lost. For example, an individual has the right to sell a house and retain up to $250,000 profit free from capital gains tax. An irrevocable trust has no such right. So if a house is likely to be sold in the next few years, it could be costly, tax-wise, to place it in Trust A.

4. Trust Paperwork

Once Trust A becomes operational (that is, when the first spouse dies), the trustee must obtain a taxpayer ID number for the trust. The trustee (typically, the surviving spouse) must also file an annual trust income tax return, IRS Form 1041. This usually isn't a big deal, but like any tax return, it requires some work.

The surviving spouse must also keep two sets of records, one for her own property, including property in Trust B, and one for Trust A property. There must be clear written evidence of which income and transactions involve the Trust A property, and which involve the property owned outright by the surviving spouse.

For many AB trusts, all you need is two separate bank or investment accounts. But if complex property holdings are involved, such as shares in a closely held S corporation or depreciated real estate holdings, you'll need a more sophisticated system.

For many older couples, these accounting and recordkeeping hassles are relatively minor annoyances. Lots of folks consider the extra hours of work well worth it to keep up to hundreds of thousands of dollars out of the hands of the IRS and in the family.

5. Potential Family Strife

An AB trust works best when everyone involved—both spouses and all final beneficiaries—understand and agree on the purposes of the trust. The primary goal is to save on overall estate tax. Usually, another goal is to give the surviving spouse the maximum allowable rights over trust property. Without this understanding, serious conflicts between the surviving spouse and the final beneficiaries may develop. Disputes are particularly likely if there are children from a prior marriage who don't support the idea of the surviving spouse having significant control over their deceased parent's property.

Put bluntly, if there is any potential for conflict between the surviving spouse and the final beneficiaries of the trust, an AB trust may well aggravate it. After all, in theory at least, there is an inherent conflict of interest between the trust's life beneficiary (the surviving spouse) and final beneficiaries (commonly, the children). The final beneficiaries may want to keep the trust principal untouched, no matter what the surviving spouse needs. On the other hand, the surviving spouse may want or need to use up most, or even all, of the trust principal.

A similar conflict can arise if the surviving spouse becomes seriously ill and can no longer serve as trustee. If a child who stands to eventually receive trust assets takes over as successor trustee, it's possible the child might be more concerned with preserving principal than with a parent's (or stepparent's) medical or other needs.

Conflicts can also occur if the final beneficiaries believe the surviving spouse, as trustee, is not managing the trust property sensibly—for example, by investing in speculative stocks or risky real estate deals. If this situation arises, there can be real trouble, possibly even a lawsuit.

An AB trust is less likely to create strife down the road if:

- Family members trust each other, are reasonably close and are able to work out any disagreements.
- The final beneficiaries understand that taking the trouble to create an AB trust is a generous act. The trust does not directly benefit the couple who creates it, but gives a big financial boost to the children, who receive substantially more of the couple's estate than they would have if the spouses had left property outright to the other.
- The final beneficiaries understand that the trust is just a tax-saving device, and support the surviving spouse's right to spend trust principal for any reason authorized by the trust document.

D. The Surviving Spouse's Rights

When it comes to dealing with the IRS, you can't have your cake and eat it, too. The property that the first spouse to die leaves in Trust A isn't taxed when the second spouse dies—but in return for this tax break, the surviving spouse never gets total control over the trust property. The surviving spouse has only the rights to Trust A property which are set out in the trust document.

Usually, however, these rights are quite broad, and this is one reason why AB trusts are so popular. If the surviving spouse couldn't exert any control over the Trust A property, most couples wouldn't be interested.

1. Rights to Income From and Use of Trust Property

Normally, the AB trust document gives the surviving spouse the right to all income the trust receives. Income could be substantial if the trust contains securities, or nonexistent if the trust owns only the house in which the surviving spouse lives.

Also, as trustee, the survivor can decide how trust property can be used. For example, the trustee decides who can live in a house owned by the trust.

The trustee is also in charge of managing trust assets. She may need to handle investments owned by the trust, such as a stock account, or buy or sell trust real estate. When making these decisions, the trustee must act in the best interests of the beneficiaries—both herself (the life beneficiary) and the final beneficiaries. In other words, the trustee isn't supposed to squander trust assets. (See Section E, below.)

2. Rights to Spend Trust Principal

Here is the source of the AB trust's flexibility. If the trust document allows it, the IRS lets the trustee spend Trust A principal for the surviving spouse's "health, education, support or maintenance." Most trust documents grant exactly those powers.

Example: *Arlo leaves his property in an AB trust with his wife Simone as the life beneficiary. Simone is the trustee and has the right to spend trust principal for her health care, education, support and maintenance. As trustee, she may sell trust property, invest it or exchange it for other property. For instance, if the trust includes a house, she could sell it and buy a retirement condo with the proceeds.*

Because trust principal can be spent for the surviving spouse's basic needs, couples can be confident that creating an AB trust will not impose financial hardship on the survivor.

Example: *Walter and Marjorie, a working couple in their 60s, own shared property worth $1.2 million. They each draft an AB trust for their half of the property. The trust document gives the survivor (as trustee) the right to spend trust principal for health care, support and maintenance.*

The survivor may never need to spend trust principal. Still, both Walter and Marjorie feel secure knowing that they will save on estate tax without tying up assets the survivor may need.

You cannot give the surviving spouse (as trustee) complete freedom to spend trust principal. If the trustee has such unlimited rights, the IRS regards the surviving spouse as the legal owner of Trust A property, and includes that property in her taxable estate at her death—exactly what you do not want.

Your trust document must use the magic words ("health, education, support or maintenance") approved by the IRS. If the document says that trust principal can be spent for, say, the "comfort" or "well-being" of the life beneficiary, there's tax trouble. The IRS would regard the trust assets as legally owned by the life beneficiary.

Example: *Pete's trust document gives his wife Sheila the right to spend Trust A principal for her "comfort." Even if she never spends a dime of the principal, the IRS will consider her the owner of the trust property and will include it in her estate at her death.*

3. The "5 and 5" Power

Another IRS-approved option is to give the trustee of an AB trust what is called a "5 and 5" power. It lets the trustee spend trust principal annually for any beneficiary, for any reason whatsoever, up to a maximum of 5% of the trust principal or $5,000, whichever is greater. You can give the trustee authority to exercise this right for the life beneficiary, the final beneficiaries or both. The trust document must specifically state which beneficiaries are eligible to receive trust property under the 5 and 5 power.

The 5 and 5 power is not in favor with many knowledgeable estate planning lawyers these days. They prefer a broader provision allowing the trustee access to principal for the life beneficiary's "health, education, support or maintenance," which protects the life beneficiary in case of real need.

One advantage of a 5 and 5 power, however, is that a final beneficiary, not just the life beneficiary, can benefit from the trust while the life beneficiary is alive. For instance, a trustee might spend some trust principal for the education of a final beneficiary. Without the 5 and 5 power, that wouldn't be possible.

The trustee is not required to exercise the 5 and 5 power. Each year it is up to the trustee to decide whether or not to give an eligible beneficiary any trust principal.

4. Restrictions on the Life Beneficiary

Most couples want the surviving spouse to have the broadest power the IRS allows to spend Trust A principal. But not everyone does. In some situations, particularly if you want to keep trust property intact for children from a prior marriage, you may not want a surviving spouse to have the right to spend trust principal. So it may come as good news that you don't have to give the trustee the power to spend Trust A principal.

Example: *Sam is in his 60s and is married to Dianne. He has two adult daughters from his former marriage. Dianne does not have children of her own. Sam's estate is worth $600,000, consisting mainly of a residence and a stock portfolio. He also has a life insurance policy that will pay $500,000 to Dianne at his death. Dianne has around $50,000 in assets.*

If he dies first, Sam wants to be sure Dianne can live comfortably, but he also wants to protect his assets for his children. Sam worries that Dianne may remarry someone who'll push her to get at the trust principal.

Sam sets up an AB trust that does not allow Dianne to spend or control the Trust A principal. (Sam also transfers ownership of his life insurance policy to Dianne, to remove the proceeds from his taxable estate and ensure that Diane will receive a substantial inheritance from him.) Sam names one daughter, not Dianne, to act as trustee of Trust A, and states flatly that the principal cannot be spent for the life beneficiary. Dianne does have the right to receive all Trust A income during her life.

Other restrictive provisions can be imposed if you wish. For example, use of Trust A property can be strictly controlled. You could give the surviving spouse the right to live in a house owned by the trust, but not to sell it or rent it out. Also, it's legal to provide that if a spouse remarries, the trust ends, and the trust property is promptly turned over to the final beneficiaries.

The surviving spouse has a right to some of your estate. *In non-community property states, a surviving spouse has the right to claim a certain portion (about a third, in most states) of the deceased spouse's estate. As long as you've left your spouse a substantial portion of your estate, or your spouse is content with what she's inherited, there will be no problem.*

Reining in the surviving spouse. *If you want to put serious restrictions on a surviving spouse, see a lawyer. A lawyer can customize the restrictions to your family and financial situation.*

E. The Trustee

For most couples, choosing a trustee for Trust A, which becomes operational when the first spouse dies, is easy. They want the surviving spouse to serve as trustee. But if your spouse is infirm, uncomfortable with financial affairs or simply uninterested, you may want to name someone else.

You'll also need to name a successor trustee for Trust A. The primary responsibility of the successor trustee will be to wind up the trust and distribute property to final beneficiaries when the surviving spouse dies. The successor trustee will also take over management of the trust property if the surviving spouse becomes incapacitated. Many people name one or more of the final beneficiaries, usually their children, as successor trustee. (See Section 5, below.)

1. The Trustee's Duties

The trustee's powers are usually set out in detail (sometimes many pages of detail) in the trust document. For example, the trustee may be given the specific power to sell trust real estate, or to buy or lease new real estate.

General legal rules also govern the trustee. Legally, the trustee is a "fiduciary," which means that she is held to the standard of highest good faith and scrupulous honesty when handling trust business (unless the trust document itself declares a lesser legal standard). For example, unless it's specifically authorized in the trust document, the trustee may not personally profit from any financial transaction involving the trust.

The trustee will most likely engage in various financial transactions on behalf of the trust. For instance, the trustee will probably deal with banks and the IRS. The trustee may also have to make investment decisions, or buy or sell trust property.

Sometimes, the trustee's actual financial responsibilities are rather simple. For example, if the primary trust asset is a valuable house, the trustee must make sure it is properly maintained, and perhaps decide whether or not to sell it.

Often, however, the trustee's work is more difficult. If much of the trust money is invested, the trustee must decide whether the investments are reasonable—neither absurdly cautious nor too risky. If the trust property includes a small business interest or a complex investment portfolio, managing the property can be a big task. For this reason, trust documents normally permit trustees to hire financial or investment advisors and pay for their advice from trust assets.

The trustee is responsible for handling all trust paperwork—for example, getting the taxpayer ID number from the IRS and keeping accurate trust financial records. Professional help can be used here if, in the trustee's judgment, it's necessary. The trustee is also responsible for having the annual trust income tax returns (state and federal) filed. If any tax is owed, the trustee must pay it from trust funds.

If someone other than the surviving spouse agrees to serve as trustee, these responsibilities may justify payment. Trust documents often allow the trustees to pay themselves "reasonable compensation" or a set amount per hour from trust property.

2. What to Look for in a Trustee

The two most important criteria to consider when choosing your trustees—both the original and successor trustee—are that you completely trust them and that they are willing to do the job.

The trustee should also have financial common sense. For instance, you want a trustee who understands the difference between a balanced, fairly conservative investment portfolio (perhaps a mix of income-oriented stock and bond funds) and a much riskier investment in someone's great idea for a new business or real estate speculation.

If you can find all this in one person, fine, but remember—your trustee can always hire investment advisors. Trustworthiness can't be bought.

Choosing your trustee may raise sensitive personal issues, matters that go beyond the hurt feelings of a child whom you don't select. For one thing, your trustee will have an ongoing relationship with the trust beneficiaries.

Example: *Malik has three children from his former marriage. He wants to leave the income from his estate to his wife, Libby, for her life, and on her death, have his estate divided equally among his children. Who should be trustee of the AB trust he creates to achieve these goals?*

Malik must carefully evaluate a number of factors:

- *The relationship between Libby and his children.*
- *Libby's willingness, if she is the sole trustee, to guard the trust principal for his children.*
- *The children's willingness, if one or more of them is chosen as trustee, to be fair to Libby and take her needs into account.*

- *The children's relationships among themselves. Will one of them sulk and make problems if he's passed over for the trustee's job?*
- *Libby and the children's ability to get along if they are co-trustees (see below), and what might happen if they can't.*

You also need to decide if your trustees will be paid for their trust work. Commonly, trustees are authorized to receive "reasonable" compensation for their labors. Often, but not invariably, trustees who are family members waive their rights to any fee.

3. Naming More Than One Trustee

Legally, you can name two, or even more, persons to serve as co-trustees. But it's usually not a good idea unless you have a compelling reason. Having multiple trustees for a trust that may last a long time can lead to serious conflict or confusion.

If you appoint co-trustees, you must decide how they will share authority—whether each can act separately for the trust or all must agree in writing to act for the trust. But even more important, you must have complete confidence that all your trustees will get along. Be cautious here. Sharing power and property can lead to unexpected results. If the co-trustees are prone to conflict, you will be doing none of them a favor by yoking them together as co-trustees.

If disagreements between co-trustees wind up in court, the trust will pay for the fight. And it will probably generate more animosity than if you had just picked one trustee in the first place and let the chips fall where they may.

4. Trust Companies and Banks as Trustees

Would you and your beneficiaries be better served if you named a professional trustee, from a bank or private trust company? Unless the trust assets are unusually complex, probably not. A trustee should have good money sense, but in most cases does not need to be an expert.

Banks can be very impersonal, perhaps paying little attention to trusts worth less than (many) millions, or treating beneficiaries as a nuisance. In addition, they charge basic management fees, and extra fees for each tiny act, that can cost a bundle.

But if there is no person you trust who is willing to serve as trustee, and you're determined to create an AB trust, you'll have to select a financial institution. Your best bet is probably to use a private trust company, a business that specializes in trust management. These companies tend to be smaller and less impersonal than banks, and more focused on trust management. If you're extremely cautious, you might even want to name another institution as an alternate trustee, in case your first choice goes out of business or decides not to handle smaller trusts. But doing this means you must go to the extra bother of making arrangements with two private trust companies.

A possible compromise is to name both an individual you trust and a financial institution as co-trustees. The hope is to get a measure of investment savvy but still have a real person in the mix. The reality may be less inviting. Many institutions won't accept a co-trustee arrangement in the first place, unless the trust is very large. And any time you appoint co-trustees, potential problems abound. (See Section 3, above.) For a run-of-the-mill AB trust, it's a better bet to name an individual trustee, who can hire good financial advisors if needed.

5. Successor Trustees

A reliable successor trustee is an essential part of an AB trust. It's the succesor trustee's job to distribute trust assets to the final beneficiaries after both spouses have died. The successor may take over sooner, while one or even both spouses are still alive, if they become incapacitated.

If you're worried that the successor trustee might die or resign before the surviving spouse dies, you can authorize an acting trustee to name, in writing, additional successor trustees. This ensures that the trustee position will remain filled even if the trustee and successor trustee you named are unable to serve.

Example: *Shannon's AB trust names her husband Bill as the trustee and her grown daughter Carolyn as the successor trustee. She also includes in the trust document a provision allowing any trustee to name, in writing, additional successor trustees.*

A few years after Shannon's death, Bill becomes very ill and can no longer serve as trustee. Carolyn takes over. To be sure the trustee position won't become vacant if something happens to her, Carolyn names her husband Phil as the next-in-line successor trustee.

F. How Much Property to Place in an AB Trust

It's up to you to decide how much of your property to leave through your AB trust.

If the total value of your property does not exceed the estate tax threshold for the year of your death (see table below), no estate tax will be due. For example, if you are the first spouse to die, and you leave $670,000 worth of property in your Trust A in 2003, there's no tax. The amount is under $700,000, the 2003 estate tax threshold.

THE FEDERAL ESTATE TAX THRESHOLD

Year of Death	Amount You Can Leave Tax-Free
1999	$650,000
2000-2001	$675,000
2002-2003	$700,000
2004	$850,000
2005	$950,000
2006 and after	$1 million

If, however, your individual estate may exceed the estate tax threshold, you need to think about how much of your property you want to leave to your AB trust. For example, if you and your mate have shared property worth $3 million, your share is worth $1.5 million. If you leave it all to your Trust A, part of it will be subject to estate tax no matter what the year of death.

To eliminate any estate tax when the first spouse dies, your trust document can specify that when you die, the value of property that's put into your Trust A must not exceed the amount that's exempt that year. The rest would go to your surviving spouse, tax-free. (The surviving spouse inherits tax-free because of the marital deduction; see Chapter 3.) For example, if you die in 2004, no more than $850,000 would be placed in your Trust A; any excess would go directly to your spouse. No tax would be due. Lawyers call this a "formula" AB trust.

Another strategy is to leave the rest of your property (over the exempt amount) in a QTIP or QDOT trust. That would also defer estate tax until the death of the second spouse, and allow you to control who inherits it after the surviving spouse dies. (See Chapter 5.)

Sometimes, however, overall estate taxes can be reduced if some tax is paid at the first death. So you may choose to leave property worth more than the estate tax threshold in your Trust A. This and your other options are discussed next.

1. Using a Formula Clause

None of us knows exactly when death will come, so we can't know in advance how large the estate tax exemption will be at our death (remember, it's going up significantly in the next few years). So if you have a large estate, you can't simply specify the maximum dollar amount of property to go into Trust A. That's where a "formula" clause comes in. It directs that the value of the assets put in Trust A equals the amount of the personal estate tax exemption for the year of death. Any property above this amount is handled by other tax-avoidance methods.

Example: *Hal, age 80, expects to leave an estate worth about $900,000 when he dies. In his AB trust document, he uses a formula clause to instruct the trustee (his widow Ellen) to place in his Trust A property worth no more than the estate tax exemption for the year of his death. The rest is left outright to Ellen.*

Hal does die first, in 2002, when the federal estate tax exemption is $700,000. So $700,000 worth of his property goes into Trust A. The other $200,000 goes to Ellen, and isn't taxed because of the marital deduction.

If Hal died in 2006, when the personal exemption will be $1 million, all $900,000 of his property would be placed in his Trust A, and nothing would go outright to Ellen.

You need consider a formula AB trust only if your half of the combined estate (yours and your spouse's) is likely to be over the estate tax threshold. If you expect your estate to be well under the threshold, you don't need a formula clause.

Using a formula AB trust can be particularly desirable if it seems likely that one spouse will long outlive the other. Leaving all property over the exemption amount to the surviving spouse, free of estate tax, gives the survivor many years to use that money. The income and potential growth in value of the assets the spouse receives can far exceed any additional estate tax that eventually must be paid. Also, the surviving spouse can take other actions to lower eventual estate tax, such as making regular tax-free gifts.

Finally, other reasons to postpone estate taxes may outweigh any higher overall tax costs. For instance, if an estate consists of property that is not liquid, such as a family-owned business or a valuable residence, paying extra tax dollars at the second death may be better than having to sell assets to get cash for tax at the first death.

2. Placing More Than the Exempt Amount in an AB Trust

Some couples, particularly elderly ones with larger estates, decide to place property worth more than the estate tax threshold in their AB trust. The reason is that the couple's overall estate tax (on both estates) can be lowered if some of their property is taxed when the first spouse dies. This result flows from the graduated estate tax rates, which start at 37% and go to 55% for estates over $3 million. The larger the estate when it is taxed, the higher the percentage that will be lost to estate tax.

Example: *Together, Carl and Sophia own shared property worth $4 million. They consider preparing an AB trust with a formula clause, directing that property equal to the amount of the personal exemption in the year of death be put in Trust A. All other property of the deceased spouse will be left to the survivor.*

Under this plan, if Carl dies in 2006, $1 million will go to his Trust A, and $1 million to Sophia outright. No estate tax will be due. If Sophia dies not long after, her estate will be $3 million, and $2 million of it will be subject to tax. (The other million will pass tax-free because of Sophia's personal exemption.)

If, however, Carl's Trust A contains all of his assets ($2 million, not just $1 million), none of it qualifies for the marital deduction. Carl's personal exemption allows $1 million to pass tax-free, and $1 million is subject to estate tax.

By increasing the value of the property in Trust A, Carl's and Sophia's estates pay a total of $691,600 in estate tax. That's $89,200 less than if only $1 million had been put in Trust A—money they have saved for their children. (Another option is to leave the excess property directly to their children instead of putting it into the AB trust; after all, Sophia will have plenty of money even without it, and less money will pile up in her estate to be taxed later.)

Estate tax on Carl's $2 million estate

	Exempt amount ($1 million) left in AB Trust, $1 million to Sophia	All assets ($2 million) left in AB trust, none to Sophia
Personal Exemption	($1 million)	($1 million)
Marital deduction	<u>($1 million)</u>	<u>-0-</u>
Tax due on	= -0-	= $1 million
Estate tax due	$0	$345,800

Estate tax on Sophia's estate

	Exempt amount ($1 million) left in AB Trust, $1 million to Sophia	All assets ($2 million) left in AB trust, none to Sophia
Value of estate	$3 million (her $2 million and $1 million from Carl)	Her $2 million (because trust property isn't counted)
Personal exemption	<u>($1 million)</u>	<u>($1 million)</u>
Tax due on	= $2 million	=$1 million
Estate tax due	$780,800	$345,800
TOTAL ESTATE TAX PAID	$780,800	$691,600

If Carl had not used an AB trust, and had just left everything to Sophia, her taxable estate would have been $4 million. After her personal $1 million tax exemption, her estate would pay $1,495,000 in tax.

3. Equalizing the Size of Each Spouse's Estate

Many couples, especially those who have been married a long time, own just about everything together: house, bank accounts, investments. But some spouses don't own equal amounts of property, and they may want to take that difference into account when setting up an AB trust.

If the value of one spouse's separate property, plus her interest in shared property, adds up to an amount large enough to owe estate tax, that spouse has estate planning decisions to make. If she leaves all her property in her Trust A when she dies, some estate tax will be owed then. If she leaves anything over the exempt amount to her husband, however, that property will pass tax-free under the marital deduction. But his estate may become large enough to be subject to estate tax at his death.

There's another option that can save money on overall estate tax: design the AB trust to equalize the worth of the two estates. This way, the wealthier spouse's estate tax rate is lowered, because the estate tax rate is lower for smaller estates. The total estate tax paid will be less.

Example: *Joe is worth $2 million; his wife, Zelda, has $800,000 in assets. Joe's estate plan places $1.4 million in his Trust A and leaves the rest to Zelda.*

Joe dies in 2003, when the estate tax exemption is $700,000. Of the $2 million he leaves, everything he leaves to Zelda ($600,000) is tax-free because of the marital deduction, and $700,000 of what he leaves to the trust is tax-free because of his personal exemption. That leaves $700,000 subject to tax.

Zelda inherits $600,000 directly, making her estate worth $1.4 million. The taxable estates of the two spouses have been roughly equalized. If Zelda dies in 2004, overall estate tax is lowered by $42,500.

Tax on Joe's $2 million estate

	$1.4 Million left in AB Trust, $600,000 to Zelda	Entire $2 Million left in AB Trust
Personal exemption	($700,000)	($700,000)
Marital deduction	($600,000)	(-0-)
Tax due on	= $700,000	= $1.4 million
Estate tax due	$283,000	$551,000

Tax on Zelda's estate in 2004

	$1.4 million (her $800,000 plus $600,000 from Joe)	$800,000 (because trust property isn't counted)
Estate		
Personal exemption	($850,000)	($850,000)
Tax due on	= $550,000	= $0
Estate tax due	$225,500	$0
TOTAL ESTATE TAX PAID	$508,500	$551,000

If you've got enough, give some directly to the kids. *Joe and Zelda might have done better by simply giving (through annual tax-free gifts) or leaving some money to their children, rather than leaving everything in the AB trust or directly to the surviving spouse.*

G. Bypass Trusts for Unmarried Persons

Anyone, whether married or not, can use a bypass trust. Like an AB trust, the trust document names a life beneficiary to receive specified rights to the trust property, and final beneficiaries to inherit the trust property when the life beneficiary dies.

You may want to consider a bypass trust if:

- You want to leave property to someone only for his or her life, then outright to others, and

- There is someone (the life beneficiary or someone else) you trust to serve as the successor trustee of the trust after you die, while the life beneficiary lives. This trustee must protect the rights of both the life beneficiary and the final beneficiaries.

1. Unmarried Couples

An unmarried couple can achieve the same overall estate tax savings with a bypass trust as can a married couple. The trust isn't usually called an AB trust, the term applied to a married couple's trust. Instead, the trust is simply called a bypass trust or a "life estate trust."

Of course, the marital deduction is not available for unmarried couples. Any amount one of them owns in excess of the personal exemption amount will be subject to estate tax when he dies, unless it's left to a tax-exempt charity. (See Chapter 6.) Still, an unmarried couple can achieve substantial estate tax savings by using a bypass trust.

Example 1: *Antonio and Gina are an unmarried couple with two grown children. Their combined assets total $1.2 million. They wish to provide support for each other for life and then leave their assets to their children. If the first to die leaves a $600,000 share outright to the other, the survivor will suddenly own all $1.2 million. That means that unless the survivor spends or gives away a lot of money, some estate tax will be due at the survivor's death (just how much depends on the year of death).*

However, if each of them creates a bypass trust and names the other as the life beneficiary, the children will eventually inherit all the property tax-free. This is because by establishing a bypass trust, both Gina's and Antonio's personal estate tax exemptions are used.

Example 2: *Terry and Tak, an unmarried couple, each own property worth $1 million. After one of them dies, they want the other to have the use of and the income from the deceased partner's property. But each also wants to preserve the bulk of their estate for other beneficiaries. Each creates a bypass trust for all his property, with income from the trust going to the other for life. Also, each authorizes the other to use any amount of trust principal for health care or basic maintenance. At the second death, remaining assets in the trust will go to their respective relatives.*

Terry dies first, in 2007, and Tak ten years later. Assuming the property values remain the same, let's look at the tax picture.

At Terry's Death in 2007:	Without a Bypass Trust (everything left to Tak)	With a Bypass Trust (everything left in trust for Tak for life, then to relatives)
Vaue of estate	$1 million	$1 million
Personal exemption	($1 million)	($1 million)
Tax due on	$0	$0
Estate tax due	$0	$0

At Tak's Death in 2017:		
Value of estate	$2 million (his $1 million and $1 million from Terry)	$1 million (because trust property not counted)
Personal exemption	($1 million)	($1 million)
Tax due on	$1 million	$0
Estate tax due	$435,000	$0

Tak never owned the $1 million left by Terry in the life estate trust, so it bypassed his estate for tax purposes. At his death, those assets pass tax-free to the relatives Terry named in his trust document. The $435,000 saved by using the bypass trust will go, eventually, to their final beneficiaries.

The savings would be even greater if, as is likely, the value of the property went up before Tak's death. For example, the value of Terry's bypass trust property might rise to $1.5 million or more. That appreciation would pass to the final beneficiaries without further tax, because the property was already taxed when Terry died.

2. Single Persons

Most single people aren't concerned with providing for another person for her or his life, then having property go to other final beneficiaries. And there is no tax trap to avoid, because there is no one other person the single person might combine his estate with, as there often is with a couple. Still, single people who want to support another person for life, then have their property benefit other younger beneficiaries, may reap big tax savings from a bypass trust. Using a bypass trust can work particularly well if the life beneficiary is elderly or won't need to spend much, if any, trust principal.

Example: *Gustav, a bachelor, leaves all of his property, worth $700,000, in a bypass trust and names his brother Ludwig as the life beneficiary. At Ludwig's death, the assets are to go to Gustav's favorite two nephews, Ludwig's sons.*

If Gustav dies before 2002, a small amount of estate tax will be due at his death. For instance, if he dies in 2000, when the estate tax threshold is $675,000, then $25,000 is subject to estate tax. If he lives longer, the estate tax threshold will have risen to more than $700,000, so no tax will be due.

The real tax savings come when Ludwig, the life beneficiary, dies. Then, the property in Gustav's trust—no matter how much it may have gone up in value—passes tax-free to Ludwig's sons. No tax is due; the trust assets have bypassed Ludwig's estate.

If Gustav simply left his property outright to Ludwig, without a bypass trust, nothing would change at Gustav's death. But when Ludwig died, Gustav's property would be added to all other property Ludwig owns, for estate tax purposes. If Ludwig's estate (including the amount he received from Gustav) was worth $1.5 million, a hefty tax would be due.

At Ludwig's Death in 2006:	*Without a Bypass Trust (everything left to Ludwig)*	*With a Bypass Trust (everything left in trust for Ludwig for life, then to nephews)*
Value of estate	*$1.5 million*	*$800,000 (because trust property not counted)*
Personal exemption	*($1 million)*	*($1 million)*
Tax due on	*= $500,000*	*= $0*
Estate tax due	*$210,000*	*$0*

Use a QTIP Trust

Estate tax laws, like many other kinds of laws, treat the married and unmarried differently. This chapter covers two tax-saving trusts available only to legally married couples: QTIPs and QDOTs.

QTIP Trusts. A QTIP (Qualified Terminable Interest Property) trust postpones estate taxes, but does not eliminate them, on property one spouse leaves to the other. For reasons explained in this chapter, QTIPs generally aren't used unless a couple's combined estate exceeds their combined estate exemptions. Couples with estates worth less than this amount—$2 million after 2005—can achieve the same goals with a simpler AB trust. (See Chapter 4.)

WHEN TO REACH FOR A QTIP		
Year of Death	Estate Tax Due If Taxable Estate Exceeds:	Consider QTIP If Couple's Combined Estate Exceeds:
1999	$650,000	$1.3 million
2000-2001	$675,000	$1.35 million
2002-2003	$700,000	$1.4 million
2004	$850,000	$1.7 million
2005	$950,000	$1.9 million
2006 and after	$1 million	$2 million

A QTIP lets you avoid paying estate tax when the first spouse dies. All property, no matter how much it's worth, left to your spouse in a QTIP is tax-free under the marital deduction. (IRC § 2056(A).) Trust property isn't taxed until the surviving spouse dies. A QTIP also lets you control where your assets go when the surviving spouse eventually dies.

Why use a QTIP rather than leave property outright to the surviving spouse? Usually because one spouse, or both, wants to be absolutely sure that his or her property eventually goes to specifically named beneficiaries, and that the surviving spouse has no power to change that.

The most common situation is when a spouse has children from a previous relationship.

QDOTs. A QDOT also postpones estate tax until the surviving spouse dies. These trusts are useful when a spouse who is not a United States citizen will inherit a large amount of property (over the estate tax threshold) from the other spouse. (See Section I, below.)

Find a knowledgeable lawyer. *To prepare a QDOT or QTIP trust, you should employ an expert estate planning lawyer. The issues and choices are complex, and a mistake in the trust document can be fatal, estate tax-wise.*

QTIPS AT A GLANCE

- A QTIP is a revocable trust. That means it's a legal entity, capable of owning property, which you set up by signing a trust document. You can revoke the QTIP trust if you change your mind later.
- A QTIP trust gives a life interest to the surviving spouse, who is entitled to:
  - receive trust income regularly
  - make use of trust assets, such as a residence, for her lifetime, within any restrictions imposed by the trust document, and
  - spend trust principal, to the extent allowed by the trust document
- In the trust document, you name final beneficiaries, who will inherit the QTIP trust assets when the surviving spouse dies.
- No estate tax is assessed when you die.
- After your death, your executor (the person in charge of carrying out the terms of your will) can evaluate the estate tax situation and choose whether or not a QTIP you've created should actually become operational. (See Section F, below.)
- When the surviving spouse dies, the net value of the property in the QTIP (as of that date) is included in her taxable estate.
- QTIP assets do not go through probate at your death or that of your spouse.

A. Do You Need a QTIP Trust?

When you leave property in a QTIP trust, all estate tax is postponed until the second spouse dies. Also, the trust usually imposes strict limits on the surviving spouse's use of trust principal. These are very desirable goals for some couples—and of no interest to others.

Many couples, particularly in first marriages, have no need of a QTIP trust. If you and your spouse own most or all of your property together and want the same people, probably your children, to eventually inherit it, then you aren't concerned with the primary purpose of a QTIP trust—letting each spouse control the final disposition of her or his property. For couples with the same final beneficiaries, it makes more sense to create an AB trust, and leave any amount over the estate tax threshold to the surviving spouse outright. (All property left outright to the surviving spouse is free from estate tax under the marital deduction. See Chapter 3.)

Example: *Miles and Suno, in their 50s, have been married for 25 years. They have two children and assets, all co-owned, worth over $4 million. They want their children to inherit their property eventually, and neither one feels the need to burden the other with the restrictions of a QTIP trust. To save on estate tax, they each create an AB trust with a "formula" clause. Under the terms of the trust, the amount of property that can pass tax-free under the estate tax exemption in the year of death will go into the AB trust; anything over that amount will go outright to the surviving spouse.*

Miles dies first, in 2002, when the estate tax exemption is $700,000. So $700,000 of his property goes into the AB trust; the rest passes directly to Suno. No estate tax is due, because the amount in the AB trust is tax-free under the personal exemption, and the rest is tax-free under the marital deduction.

If you do not want your surviving spouse to have unlimited control over any of your assets, you won't want to leave property outright to him or her. But you may well, as many couples do, want your spouse to at least receive income from your property and also to avoid paying any estate tax on that property as long as your spouse lives. This is precisely what a QTIP trust achieves. In other words, a QTIP trust allows you to have the trust property treated, tax-wise, as if the surviving spouse had inherited it outright, (in other words, it qualifies for the marital deduction), but without giving up control over the property's ultimate disposition.

QTIPs are commonly used by older, prosperous spouses who have children from earlier marriages. Often, a QTIP is used in addition to an AB trust. That's because an AB trust shields from tax only an amount up to the estate tax threshold. A QTIP postpones (but doesn't eliminate, remember) tax on any amount.

Example: *Betty dies in 2003, leaving an estate worth $1 million. Her husband and grown children survive her.*

Here are the different tax results at her death, depending on whether or not she uses a QTIP trust in addition to an AB trust.

	$1 million in AB trust	*$700,000 in AB trust, $300,000 in QTIP trust*
Personal estate tax exemption	*($700,000)*	*($700,000)*
Marital deduction	*($0)*	*($300,000)*
Tax due on	*$300,000*	*$0*
Estate tax due	*$116,000*	*$0*

Each member of a couple can create separate AB and QTIP trusts, so each one can use his or her personal estate tax exemption. The usual plan is for each spouse to create an AB trust, to be funded with property worth up to the personal estate tax exemption (a "formula" trust; see Chapter 4) and a QTIP trust to postpone payment of estate tax on anything over that amount. The spouses name each other as life beneficiaries of each trust; each also chooses his or her final beneficiaries. When the first spouse dies, property worth up to the amount of the personal exemption for that year is placed in the AB trust and is exempt from estate tax. All that spouse's remaining property goes into the QTIP trust, which is also exempt from tax.

Using a QTIP lets you preserve property for children from a former relationship, or for any other final beneficiaries you want to name. Commonly, the surviving spouse is given very restricted rights to spend trust principal, or no rights at all.

Example: *Michael, who is in his 70s, has assets worth $1.5 million when he marries Angela, his second wife. She has very little property of her own. If Michael dies before Angela does, he wants to be sure she is provided for, but he also wants to ensure that his children from his first marriage eventually inherit his property.*

Michael considers creating an AB trust for the amount of his personal estate tax exemption, and simply leaving anything over that amount to his children. But that plan has two drawbacks. First, Michael thinks that Angela may need all the income his $1.5 million will provide. Second, property left directly to the children would be taxed at his death.

So Michael creates a QTIP trust for all his assets over the estate tax threshold at his death. Angela is the life beneficiary and will receive all trust income for as long as she lives. Michael decides she will have no right whatsoever to spend trust principal. Michael designates his children as the trust's final beneficiaries, to receive the principal when Angela dies.

It's important to keep in mind that a QTIP does not eliminate any estate taxes. It simply postpones taxes due on QTIP property until the surviving spouse dies. When that spouse dies, the full value of the property, as of the date of that spouse's death, is included in that spouse's taxable estate. If the property has gone up significantly in value, more estate tax may be paid than if the QTIP property had been included in the estate of the first spouse to die. (See Section C, below.)

QTIP trusts also raise personal issues. If you're considering a QTIP trust, and you have children from a former marriage, think about how you will balance their interests and those of your current spouse. The solution depends on your unique situation. Among other things, you must decide what rights, if any, your spouse will have to spend trust principal, and who should serve as trustee of the trust. These and other family concerns are discussed below.

B. How QTIP Trusts Work

A QTIP works much like an AB trust, in some ways. Each spouse can create a separate QTIP trust for his or her property, including shares of co-owned property. Under IRS regulations, the surviving spouse receives all the income from the QTIP trust but, as we've seen, has no power over final distribution of that property. Each spouse chooses his or her final QTIP beneficiaries, who will inherit the trust property after the surviving spouse's death.

Only one of a couple's QTIP trusts will ever become operational— that of the first spouse to die. The property that would have gone into the surviving spouse's QTIP is simply distributed, at that spouse's death, outright to the final beneficiaries.

Sometimes only one member of a couple creates a QTIP, because the other owns relatively little property, and is not concerned with estate taxes or supporting the other spouse.

Example *Li-shan has assets worth $1.6 million. Her husband Talbot owns property worth $125,000. It's her second marriage, his fourth. They agree that if she survives him, she won't need any of his property to live on. They also agree that if he survives her, he will need income from her estate.*

Talbot leaves his property outright to his two grandchildren. Li-shan creates a more complex plan, leaving the amount of the personal exemption at her death in an AB trust and the balance in a QTIP trust, with her husband as life beneficiary of both trusts. He has no rights to spend the principal of either. Because Talbot is elderly and has never been very good at practical matters, Li-shan names her eldest child as trustee of both trusts.

When Li-shan dies in 2003, $700,000 is placed in her AB trust, and $900,000 into the QTIP. No federal estate tax is due. Property in the QTIP trust is exempt because it qualifies for the unlimited marital deduction.

C. A Drawback of QTIP Trusts: Possible Higher Eventual Tax

As you may be tired of hearing by now, estate tax on property left in a QTIP trust is not eliminated—it's just postponed. When the second spouse dies, all property in that spouse's estate is subject to estate tax. Under tax law, the estate includes all property in the QTIP, valued as of the date of the surviving spouse's death.

Example: *Sheila leaves property worth $2.5 million in a QTIP, with Atah, her husband, as life beneficiary. No tax is due at her death. Atah has an estate of $500,000 of his own. When he dies, his total estate, now including property in the QTIP, is worth $3 million. He dies in 2006, when the personal estate tax exemption is $1 million, so $2 million will be taxed.*

The problem, from an estate tax viewpoint, is that the full value of the QTIP property is included in the taxable estate of the second spouse to die. That means the total tax paid can be higher than if the first spouse had left that property by other methods.

Example: *Gregor leaves $500,000 in an AB trust and creates a QTIP trust for his wife, Natalie, with his children as final beneficiaries. When Gregor dies, $1.5 million is placed in the QTIP. Natalie has an estate of $1 million. Here's the tax situation when Natalie dies:*

Natalie's separate estate	*$1 million*
Property inherited from Gregor in QTIP	*+ $1.5 million*
Natalie's total estate	*$2.5 million*

Because the bigger the estate, the higher the estate tax rates, the total tax paid on this $2.5 million will be higher than the total paid if the two estates had been taxed separately.

Perhaps you've noticed that we've been making an assumption: that the value of the property in a QTIP trust stays the same from the time the first spouse dies until the surviving spouse dies. In reality, this is often not so, especially if the surviving spouse lives for more than a few years longer. The QTIP property is likely to go up in value, perhaps substantially. If that occurs, the increase is also subject to estate tax when the surviving spouse dies.

Example: *Ivan creates a QTIP trust with property that is worth $1.1 million when he dies. By the time his wife, Olga, dies 12 years later, the value of the trust property has risen to $3.6 million. The whole $3.6 million is included in Olga's taxable estate.*

By contrast, property left in an AB trust is valued, for tax purposes, only once, when the first spouse dies. If the trust assets later go up in value, the increase is not taxed when the second spouse dies.

QTIPs do not, however, always cost couples in the long run, for several reasons:

- A surviving spouse who outlives the other by at least a few years will receive income from *all* the deceased spouse's property; none of that property is used to pay estate tax. The additional income may exceed any additional tax paid when the second spouse dies.
- If the surviving spouse is given the right to spend trust principal and does so, the value of the trust property may be reduced.
- If a surviving spouse has few assets of his own, using a QTIP may actually reduce overall estate taxes, by making the estates of each spouse closer in value.

Example: *Phyllis has an estate of $1.4 million. Her second husband, Jack, has little money (but a lot of flair, and love for her). Phyllis dies in 2002, leaving $700,000 in an AB trust. She leaves the rest, $700,000, in a QTIP.*

Jack dies in 2006, when the estate tax exemption is $1 million. His own estate is worth $25,000. The value in the property of the QTIP has grown to $800,000. The total value of property subject to tax when Jack dies is $825,000, well under the estate tax exemption for 2006, so no tax is paid.

By contrast, if Phyllis had left all her property in the AB trust, $700,000 would have been subject to tax.

D. The Surviving Spouse's Rights

If you create a QTIP trust, IRS rules mandate that the surviving spouse be given two important rights:

- the right to receive all income from property in the QTIP trust, and
- the right to require that the trustee sell non-income-producing property and invest the proceeds in income-producing property.

If the spouse doesn't have these rights, the IRS will rule that the QTIP property doesn't qualify for the marital deduction—and estate taxes won't be postponed.

1. The Right to Receive All Trust Income

There are no exceptions to the rule that a surviving spouse must receive all of the income from a QTIP—even if neither spouse wants it this way. The trustee (often, the surviving spouse) must distribute all income at least once a year to the spouse, who must pay tax on it as ordinary income. Income cannot stay in the trust. If the surviving spouse becomes incapacitated, the trustee must spend the income for the spouse's benefit.

As long as the surviving spouse lives, the trustee of a QTIP trust cannot spend any of the principal or income from the trust for the benefit of anyone else. This rule is intended to protect both the surviving spouse, who receives a continuing income, and the final beneficiaries, who will eventually receive the trust principal.

Occasionally these restrictions can be troublesome. For example, suppose the surviving spouse remarries or no longer really needs the trust income. The spouse might want to end the trust and have the principal distributed to the final beneficiaries. But that can't be done. A QTIP trust cannot end until the second spouse dies.

Or suppose that one of the final beneficiaries really needs money, and the surviving spouse wants to give it from the trust income or principal. Sorry, can't be done. A surviving spouse who wants to help out must do so indirectly. Because all trust income is hers to do with as she wishes, she can give all or part of it to the needy final beneficiary. But legally, she's making a gift, subject to gift tax if it exceeds the amount of the annual gift tax exclusion. She cannot channel principal directly to the final beneficiary.

Example: *Alice directs that a QTIP trust be created at her death, with the income going to her husband, Mark. She does not grant him the right to spend trust principal. At Mark's death, the assets of the trust will pass to her five children from two previous marriages.*

Mark has a substantial estate himself, and several years after Alice dies, he remarries a very wealthy woman. He would like to end the trust, but he can't. All trust income continues to go to him.

Meanwhile, Alice's oldest son, Edward, desperately needs money to keep his business afloat. Mark gives Edward income from the trust as he receives it, but it isn't enough. The business fails—hardly what Alice would have wanted.

2. Selling Property That Doesn't Produce Income

You can put any kind of property into a QTIP—a house, furniture, money, stock, even a business—but the surviving spouse must have the right to demand that it be converted into a form of property that produces income. So if the trust includes a safe deposit box full of gold coins or a collection of valuable antique chairs, the surviving spouse can insist they be sold and the proceeds invested in income-producing securities.

Example: *Gretchen creates a QTIP trust with her husband, Lloyd, as the life beneficiary. The trust assets consist of stocks, bonds, a residence and a vacation home. After Gretchen's death, Lloyd decides that the income is not enough for him to live on in the manner he's used to. Using his authority as life beneficiary and trustee, he sells the vacation home and invests the proceeds in bonds that yield income.*

IRS REQUIREMENTS FOR A VALID QTIP TRUST

To qualify as a valid QTIP trust under federal law (IRC § 2056(b)(7)), the trust document must contain these provisions:

1. All income from the trust must be distributed to the surviving spouse at least annually.
2. The spouse can demand that trust property be converted to income-producing property.
3. No one, not even the surviving spouse, may spend principal for the benefit of anybody but the spouse.

E. Powers That May Be Given to the Surviving Spouse

The IRS allows—but does not require—other powers to be included in a QTIP. Here is a look at the three most important ones.

1. Power to Spend Trust Principal

You have great flexibility when it comes to giving the surviving spouse access to trust principal. The surviving spouse is considered, for estate tax purposes, the owner of all property in the QTIP. That means she can be given the right to spend (invade) trust principal for her benefit for any reason she wants, for any amount she wants. (This is another way in which a QTIP trust differs from an AB trust.)

It's rare, however, to grant such unlimited power to spend trust principal. After all, it would be essentially the same as leaving the property outright to the surviving spouse. If that's what you want, just do it directly, and no estate tax will be imposed at your death because of the marital deduction. Most people who go to the trouble of making a QTIP trust do it to impose some restrictions on the surviving spouse, to protect the principal for the final beneficiaries.

Sometimes the surviving spouse is given no right to spend trust principal, period. Other QTIP trusts let a spouse use principal only if it's necessary for:

- emergency health care, or
- the surviving spouse's "education, health care, support or maintenance." (This is the standard commonly used in AB trusts.)

In many instances, the surviving spouse serves as trustee of the QTIP trust. If, however, you grant your spouse broad powers to spend principal, you may want to name a disinterested party as trustee or co-trustee. The person you name will be responsible for making sure that spending meets the criteria set out in the trust document—and for reassuring the final beneficiaries that the rules are being followed. Of course, you may want to name someone else as trustee for any number of reasons, from the fragility of your spouse to a belief that someone else would better manage the trust assets. (See Section H, below.)

Stave off family fights by being very clear about the spouse's rights. *If the surviving spouse can spend trust principal, there's an inherent risk of conflict between the spouse and the final beneficiaries. Make the trust document very specific about the spouse's rights. The last thing you want is a fight over what assets can and cannot be used, or what standard the spouse must meet to justify spending principal.*

2. The "5 and 5" Power

Another way to give the surviving spouse access to some trust principal is to use something called the "5 and 5" power. It gives the spouse the right to take out $5,000 or 5% of the trust principal, whichever is greater, each year. There are no restrictions on how the surviving spouse can spend this money.

The surviving spouse does not have to use this right in any one year. But if it is not used in one year, that year's right is lost. In other words, the right is not cumulative, year to year.

Example: *Isabelle is the trustee and life beneficiary of a QTIP trust established by her late husband. The trust document includes a 5 and 5 power. If she doesn't exercise the right this year, she cannot take an extra 5% or $5,000 out of the trust principal next year.*

The 5 and 5 power is not used much these days. Usually, people prefer to spell out the reasons the spouse can spend principal, and not try to restrict the amount.

3. The Power to Distribute Trust Property Among a Group of Beneficiaries

With a QTIP trust, you can choose a group of possible final beneficiaries, but let your surviving spouse decide how much each one actually inherits from the trust. It's not a widely used strategy, but it can be a good one if you trust your spouse's judgment and expect him or her to outlive you by many years.

This power can be helpful because it's impossible to know, now, what each of your children might need 10, 20 or even 30 years from now. A surviving spouse who lives for many years will be in a far better position to determine who, of the group of final beneficiaries you chose, needs what. For example, one child may have completely dedicated herself to the family business, another may have big medical expenses and yet another may have amassed such wealth that he needs less than the others.

In legal terms, the spouse has a "limited power of appointment" over the assets in the trust. The power can extend over some or all of the trust assets.

Example: *Sara is married to Emmanuel, nine years younger than she is. Sara fully trusts Emmanuel and is confident he loves her two children, Alison and Lori, from a prior marriage. When Sara prepares her QTIP, Alison has two young children (and wants more) and Lori is single. Sara wants to provide for her daughters but also leave direct gifts to her grandchildren.*

She names her children and grandchildren as the final beneficiaries of her QTIP trust. She provides that each daughter will receive 30% of the trust property, and that the remaining 40% will be divided among all her grandchildren when final distribution of the trust assets is made. She doesn't want to specify the precise divisions now because there may be (she hopes) additional grandchildren. And if Emmanuel survives her by a considerable time, she believes he will be in a far better position to decide how much money to leave to each grandchild. So she gives Emmanuel authority to make the decision.

If the trust grants your surviving spouse the power to decide how to distribute trust property among your beneficiaries, he or she makes the decision and leaves instructions in a living trust or will.

F. The Executor's Role: Making the "QTIP Election"

The IRS imposes one final requirement for creating a valid QTIP: The executor of the deceased spouse's estate must choose, on the federal estate tax return, to have part or all of the trust be treated as a QTIP.

This means that although you can set up a QTIP trust to take effect at your death, tax law doesn't allow you to make the final decision about whether or not the trust actually becomes operational. That's up to your executor, the person named in your will to wind up your affairs. The choice, called the QTIP election, is made on your federal estate tax return, due nine months after your death. (A return must be filed for any estate where the gross value exceeds the estate tax exemption for the year of death. Even if no tax will be due at your death, a return must still be filed.) If the executor doesn't make the QTIP election properly, no valid QTIP trust exists, period.

DOING THE PAPERWORK

Making the QTIP election itself amounts to marking the correct box on the estate tax return and then listing the property that is to go into the trust. Seems simple, but mistakes are made. In one case, an executor forgot to mark the right box and then sought IRS permission to file an amended return electing a QTIP. Nope, said the IRS, which sometimes seems to delight in denying a proposed QTIP trust eligibility for the marital deduction and insisting that estate tax be paid immediately.

To make a smart decision, the executor must figure out which course will result in the smallest estate tax bill. The executor has several choices:

- Decide not to elect the QTIP at all.
- Elect that all property left in the (possible) QTIP trust actually be treated as QTIP property.
- Elect to have only a portion of the designated property treated as a QTIP.

These options make possible a great deal of strategic after-death tax planning. But in some family situations, it can require the wisdom of Solomon, not to mention high-quality tax advice, to make the best choice.

1. No QTIP Election

Why would an executor choose to scrap a carefully planned QTIP trust? Because in larger estates, it may lower estate taxes to include possible QTIP trust property in the taxable estate of the deceased spouse instead of having it receive QTIP treatment.

If electing the QTIP would result in the surviving spouse's estate being much larger than that of the first spouse to die, higher overall estate tax would eventually be paid. In such a case, the executor might decide to go ahead and pay any estate tax assessed against the first spouse's property. The tax rate would be lower on this amount of property than it would be if it were combined, for estate tax purposes, with the surviving spouse's. The surviving spouse would have to make some tax payments now in exchange for overall tax savings later.

Usually, the surviving spouse is also the executor, and is in charge of making the QTIP decision. But if the surviving spouse isn't the executor, and the two disagree, there can be a real power struggle. Legally, it's up to the executor.

2. Partial QTIP Election

Another option is to have only some of the deceased spouse's property receive QTIP treatment. For example, the executor could elect to have only 60% of the trust property treated as a QTIP. The remaining 40% may be subject to estate tax now, depending on who inherits it. This is called a partial QTIP election.

An executor can make a partial QTIP election only in terms of a percentage or fraction of the total property originally left for the QTIP. For example, an executor can elect to have 40% or 63% or one-third of the total property originally left for the QTIP actually qualify for QTIP tax treatment. What the executor cannot do is specify that particular assets be included in or excluded from the QTIP. The IRS simply doesn't allow it.

Estate planners seldom recommend partial QTIP elections, and most people who create QTIPs, and their executors, don't bother with them. They're just too worky and complicated. For example, you can imagine the paperwork if 75% of your house gets QTIP treatment and 25% doesn't. Also, splitting things up this way can complicate matters like real estate tax or refinancing.

But when assets are liquid (marketable securities, for·example), a partial QTIP election may be a reasonable way to lower overall estate tax. Any percentage of the trust property that doesn't receive QTIP treatment still must, under IRS rules, be used for the surviving spouse's benefit. It's still held in trust, and it can't go to anyone else. Nothing changes except the tax treatment: Estate tax is not deferred on the portion not elected.

Making a partial QTIP election, instead of a full one, can make a big difference, tax-wise.

Example: *Brian has an estate worth $2 million. His wife Gloria has her own property worth $2 million. Brian leaves his $2 million in a QTIP for Gloria, with the income to go to her and the assets to go later to the children from his first marriage. Brian dies in 2006, when the personal estate tax exemption is $1 million.*

Here's a look at the very different tax consequences that result if Brian's executor chooses a full QTIP election or a partial one:

	Full QTIP Treatment	Partial (50%) QTIP Treatment
At Brian's death:		
Brian's gross estate	$2 million	$2 million
Property given marital deduction because of QTIP treatment	($2 million)	($1 million)
Personal tax exemption	*not used*	*($1 million)*
Estate tax due on	-0-	-0-
Estate tax due	-0-	-0-
At Gloria's death:		
Gloria's estate	$4 million	$3 million
Personal tax exemption	($1 million)	($1 million)
Estate tax due on	$3 million	$2 million
Estate tax due	$1,495,000	$930,000

By electing to have only half of the trust property qualify for the QTIP, $565,000 that would have gone to pay estate tax is saved for the final beneficiaries. The savings is possible because of the graduated estate tax. Electing a full QTIP would cause the second estate to be taxed at 55%. But with half of it subject to taxation at Brian's death (and exempt from tax because of the personal tax exemption), both Brian's and Gloria's estates fall into a lower bracket, only 41%.

A number of factors can contribute to the decision your executor makes regarding the QTIP election. One big factor is that changed circumstances since you prepared the QTIP trust may mean the trust is no longer financially desirable.

Example: *Steve owns property worth about $1 million. He drafts a QTIP trust for $900,000 of his assets and an AB trust for the remaining $100,000. His wife, Esther, has property of her own worth about $200,000. She will get the income from both trusts, and the principal from both will go to Steve's son, Zack, at Esther's death.*

Several years later, Esther inherits property worth $450,000, making her own assets worth $650,000. Steve neglects to revise his estate plan. When Steve dies in 2006, if the QTIP trust goes into effect, Esther's taxable estate will be worth over $1.5 million—well over the personal exemption amount.

Steve's executor looks at the whole picture and decides not to make a QTIP election that would postpone taxes. This means that the $900,000 Steve had earmarked for QTIP treatment will still go into the trust, subject to the terms of the QTIP. But tax will not be deferred. The property will be subject to estate tax immediately, but no tax is due because of Steve's personal exemption. Esther will still get the income from both trusts, and Zack will still inherit the principal when she dies.

G. The Reverse QTIP Election

Here's another possible twist that may be useful if the final beneficiaries of your QTIP trust are your grandchildren.

Start by understanding that all assets that are left by a grandparent to a grandchild or other member of that generation (skipping the middle generation) are subject to an extra tax, called the Generation-Skipping Transfer Tax or GSTT. There is, however, an automatic $1 million exemption from this tax. A procedure called the "reverse QTIP election" can ensure that you and your spouse make full use of this exemption.

If the final beneficiaries of a QTIP trust (the people who inherit trust property when the surviving spouse dies) are more than one generation away from the person who created the trust, the law considers the surviving spouse (the life beneficiary) the one transferring the property for GSTT purposes. However, when the first spouse's executor makes a reverse QTIP election, the first spouse to die is considered the giver. This preserves that first spouse's $1 million GSTT exemption. The second spouse can transfer another million to grandchildren free of the GSTT.

This reverse QTIP election is concerned only with the Generation-Skipping Transfer Tax. It is an entirely separate matter from the basic QTIP election, where the executor decides whether or not to use a QTIP, and if so, how much property to actually place in the QTIP trust.

H. Choosing Your Trustee

After all this, you undoubtedly see that choosing the right person to serve as trustee of your QTIP is vital. The trustee will manage the trust property from your death until it's turned over to the final beneficiaries.

Many people name the surviving spouse, but a grown child or someone else entirely can serve as co-trustee or sole trustee. There's no one-size-fits-all answer.

If you plan to choose your spouse, first ask yourself a few questions:

- Do you fully trust your spouse to protect the trust principal, your final beneficiaries' inheritance?
- Do your final beneficiaries feel the same way?
- Do you think that one of your children (and not your spouse) has the wisdom to best balance the needs of the surviving spouse against the rights of the final beneficiaries?

In making your decision, consider trustworthiness and competence. You should have complete faith that the person you choose will carry out your wishes and that he or she has the financial savvy to do the job. Don't discount your gut feelings. Given family dynamics—sibling rivalry, for example—the best choice from a business standpoint isn't always the best choice to maintain family harmony.

Remember also that the executor of your will must decide whether or not property in the trust should actually receive QTIP treatment. So it's common to have your QTIP trustee be the same person as your executor.

I. Trusts for Non-Citizen Spouses: QDOTs

An alternative to a QTIP, if you are married to someone who is not a citizen of the United States, is something called a QDOT. The concern a QDOT addresses is that property left to your non-citizen spouse is not eligible for the unlimited marital deduction. So if you leave property worth more than the personal exemption amount, it will be subject to tax, even if some or all of it goes to your non-citizen spouse. (See Chapter 3.)

You can, however, defer estate tax on property left to a non-citizen spouse with a QDOT, or "Qualified Domestic Trust." All property, no matter how much it's worth, left to a non-citizen spouse in a QDOT is tax-free under the marital deduction. (IRC § 2056(A).) Trust property isn't taxed until the non-citizen spouse dies.

Some special rules apply to these trusts. The surviving spouse cannot be the sole trustee; at least one of the trustees must be either a U.S. citizen or a U.S. corporation. And the surviving spouse must be entitled to receive all income from the trust. Finally, if any trust principal is distributed to the non-citizen spouse during her life, estate tax is assessed on it. The only exception to this rule is in cases of "hardship"—

immediate needs relating to health, maintenance, education or support that cannot be met by other reasonable means. The IRS approves hardship exemptions on a case-by-case basis.

When the surviving non-citizen spouse dies, the full value of the QDOT trust assets, as of the date of death, is subject to estate tax.

Example: *Juan, a U.S. citizen, has assets of $2 million. He is married to Maria, who is a legal resident of the United States but not a citizen. Juan's estate plan includes an outright bequest to Maria of the amount that is exempt from federal estate tax under Juan's personal exemption. The remaining assets will go into a QDOT for Maria's benefit during her life, and will be distributed, at her death, to their children. Juan appoints his brother Ricardo, a U.S. citizen, to serve as co-trustee with Maria.*

At Juan's death, no estate tax is due because of the personal tax exemption and the QDOT. Maria will receive all of the income from the trust for her life; if she receives principal, it will be subject to estate tax immediately. At Maria's death, whatever is still in the trust will be taxed.

The QDOT rules provide an incentive to a non-citizen spouse to become a U.S. citizen. If the spouse becomes a citizen before the deceased spouse's estate tax return is filed (generally, nine months after the death) or before receiving any trust principal, property in the trust receives the full marital deduction, and assets may be spent during the spouse's lifetime without paying estate tax.

A QDOT can even be created after the citizen spouse's death. If someone who is married to a non-citizen prepared a trust before the federal QDOT law went into effect in 1988, or just didn't know about the law, the surviving non-citizen spouse can ask the IRS to let the estate plan be "reformed" to meet the guidelines for a QDOT.

The QDOT must be "elected" by the executor of the deceased spouse's estate on the estate tax return, due nine months after the death. If the executor doesn't do this correctly, the QDOT won't legally exist.

Example: *Sol is married to Rosalie and has two children from a previous marriage. His estate is worth $1.7 million. He creates a QTIP trust for $1 million. All of the income from the trust will be paid to Rosalie for her lifetime, and at her death the trust assets will go to his children. Rosalie has the right to spend trust principal only for medical care and basic support (food, housing), and then only if her other assets are insufficient. Rosalie gets along well with Sol's children, and Sol trusts her to protect their interests (the trust principal), so he appoints her as trustee.*

Sol also leaves $350,000 outright to each child. No estate tax will be due on this $700,000 (if Sol dies after 2001) because of Sol's personal estate tax exemption. And of course, no taxes will be due on the QDOT property when Sol dies. At Rosalie's death, the trust principal will be counted as part of her taxable estate.

What can you do if you want to leave a large estate to a non-citizen spouse? Of course, your spouse might consider acquiring U.S. citizenship. But that's not always feasible, and at the least, it will take a while.

First, it's important to understand that the personal estate tax exemption is available to each spouse, regardless of citizenship. So you can leave a non-citizen spouse $650,000 to $1 million tax-free, depending on the year of death. Any amount over that is subject to estate tax.

CHAPTER 6

Give to Charity

Americans support more than a million different nonprofit organizations, formed to do everything from save souls to save the local creek. In 1997, Americans contributed more than $143 billion to nonprofits, according to the American Association of Fund-Raising Counsel. If you want to make a substantial gift to a charity, you may find that your good deed gives you not only a sense of satisfaction, but some big tax breaks as well.

Giving to charity can save on taxes in several ways:

- **Gift/estate tax.** Property you give or leave to a tax-exempt charity, regardless of value, isn't subject to the gift/estate tax.

- **Income tax.** You can deduct the full value of charitable gifts, though not necessarily in one year.

- **Capital gains tax.** If you have property that has increased in value since you acquired it, you may want to transfer it to a charity, using a charitable trust. The charity can sell it without incurring capital gains tax, and can then pay you income based on the sale price of the property.

You can give to charity while you're alive or at your death; either way will save on estate tax. If you have a fairly big chunk of money to give away, you may want to explore charitable trusts. They can provide retirement income as well as tax savings.

THE SCHOOL FOR GIVING

Charitable giving can be complicated—especially if you're rolling in money and are befuddled by too many options. For people with that happy problem, foundations and other nonprofits are offering seminars and courses in the finer points of giving. ("The Very Rich Learn to Give Their Money Away," *New York Times*, May 3, 1998, p. 1.)

You can pay for these organizations' advice and experience by the hour, or attend a weekend seminar. Or, if you're really among the high rollers, check out the Rockefeller Foundation's course in Practical Philanthropy. With a $20,000 price tag, it will get you in the habit of sharing your wealth.

A. Investigating Charities: Look Before They Reap

Before you plan to make a big gift to an organization, you'll probably want to do some homework. You want to be sure that your gift will qualify for a tax deduction—and that the money will be used for the programs you want to support.

1. Are Contributions Tax-Deductible?

First, you need to know whether or not the organization has been blessed by the IRS with tax-deductible status. It can be confusing, but donations to some tax-exempt organizations are **not** tax-deductible. Only charities with the IRS stamp of approval will make it possible for you to get income and estate tax benefits. All the familiar big charities, and many small local ones, qualify; if you aren't sure about an organization you have your eye on, find out.

There are several ways to discover whether or not deductions to a charity will be tax-deductible. The charity itself or a charity rating organization (several are listed below) can tell you. So can the IRS, which publishes a list of more than half a million approved public charities. So whether you're interested in the Central Illinois Watch and Clock Collectors or the Cudahy, Wisconsin Library Expansion Committee, it's on the IRS list.

You can find the IRS list online or get it in print as IRS Publication 78. To view it online, go to www.irs.gov/prod/search/eosearch.html.

2. How the Charity Operates

Once you've answered the threshold tax-deductibility question, you'll also want to find out just where your money will go. Be sure that the organization will spend it on programs to carry out the mission you want to support, not primarily to raise more funds or pay administrators handsomely. Some charities hire professional fundraising companies that keep as much as 80% of the money they raise.

There are lots of ways to check out the workings of charities you're interested in. To see exactly how a charity spends its money, you can ask it for a copy of its annual report.

Several organizations also publish their ratings of charities, evaluating them based on the percentage of funds used for programs, fundraising and administration. Here are some places to start:

- The GuideStar site, at www.guidestar.org, analyzes a huge number—more than 600,000—of charitable organizations. It also publishes a *Guide for the Responsible Donor* and information for nonprofits. GuideStar is a project of Philanthropic Research, Inc., which says its goal is to give donors and others objective information about charities. You can contact Philanthropic Research, Inc. at 1126 Professional Dr., Williamsburg, VA 23185, (757) 229-4631.

- The National Charities Information Bureau, which aims to promote informed giving, offers tips for donors and reports on many specific charities. Find it at www.give.org. You can order the NCIB's free *Wise Giving Guide* online or by writing to the NCIB at 19 Union Square West, Dept. 326, New York, NY 10003.

- *The Giver's Charity Rating Guide* evaluates charities and lists the percentage of their funds that actually goes for charitable services. It's $3 from the American Institute of Philanthropy, 4579 Laclede Ave., Suite E17, St. Louis, MO 63103, (301) 913-5200.

B. Making Outright Gifts: What to Give

When most people give to charity, they simply take out their check-books or credit cards and sign over some money, perhaps feeling a bit better about themselves and the world that day. Although cash may be the easiest gift, giving other kinds of property can also help out a favorite charity and improve your own tax situation. Here are some ideas for you to consider.

NO PROOF, NO DEDUCTION

To get a large charitable deduction claim past IRS scrutiny, you must have written proof of the gift by the time you file your income tax return.

Gifts of $250 or more. You must get a written acknowledgment of your gift from the charity at the time you make the gift. (IRC § 170(f)(8)(C).) Most charities are well aware of this rule and will promptly send you a letter or receipt. If you don't get one, ask.

Gifts worth $5,000 or more. If you give property (other than publicly traded securities) and claim a charitable deduction of more than $5,000, you must get an appraisal before you file your tax return. And you must attach to your return a summary of the appraisal. Use IRS Form 8283, Noncash Charitable Contributions.

1. Securities

Among people who know something about taxes, securities are a popular gift, and for good reason. Giving away stocks and bonds that have gone up in value since you acquired them can benefit everyone: you, your family and the charity. Here's why:

- You pay no capital gains tax at the sale of the securities, because the charity, not you, sells them—and charities aren't liable for capital gains tax.

- On your income tax return, you can take a charitable deduction for the fair market value of the securities when you give them, if you've held them for at least a year.

- The charitable deduction can be as much as 30% of your adjusted gross income in the year you make the gift. Any excess deductions can be taken over the next five years. (The rules are explained in Section F, below.)

2. Life Insurance Policies

If you own a life insurance policy at your death, the proceeds are included in your taxable estate—and a policy that pays several hundred thousand dollars can bump up the estate tax bill considerably. There are two ways to get the policy proceeds out of your taxable estate and make a charitable gift at the same time.

One option is to name the charity as the beneficiary (or one beneficiary) of the policy. If you've been keeping up a policy for many years, re-examine your family situation: If your children are grown and independent, and your spouse doesn't rely on your income, you may want to let a charity have the policy proceeds after your death.

The second method is to give ownership of the policy itself to the charity right now. Giving away life insurance policies is discussed in detail in Chapter 7.

3. Bank and Retirement Accounts

It's very easy to arrange for a charity to inherit your Individual Retirement Account (traditional or Roth IRA) or the funds in bank accounts or Certificates of Deposit.

If you want to leave your retirement account funds to charity, simply designate the charity as the beneficiary, on a form provided by the account administrator. The charity will inherit whatever funds are in the account at your death.

For bank accounts, there's a similar process. All you have to do is turn these accounts into "payable-on-death" (P.O.D.) accounts, by filling out a short form at the bank. Simply name the charity as the P.O.D. payee. You can revoke the designation at any time, so you're not actually making a gift now, and there are no gift tax consequences. The gift will be made at your death.

An added bonus: The funds in a retirement account or payable-on-death bank account do not go through probate. The charity can claim them quickly and easily.

If you're married, be careful with a 401(k) account. *A special rule applies to 401(k) retirement accounts: Your spouse must be the beneficiary unless he or she gives up this right, in writing. Your fund administrator can give you the necessary form for your spouse to sign, if that's what you both want.*

4. Real Estate

You can donate a house, farm, office building or undeveloped land to a charity. If the value of the property has gone up since you acquired it, you'll avoid paying capital gains tax. If you're donating your home, the charity will be happy to work out an arrangement that lets you and your spouse live there for the rest of your lives, with the property passing to the charity only at your death. The charity gets a valuable gift, and the value of your home won't be included in your taxable estate.

Contracts involving real estate should be drawn up carefully, paying careful attention to your unique circumstances. You'll want your own lawyer involved.

C. Charitable Trusts

Charitable trusts can be wonderful estate planning tools. Used intelligently, they can give you income for life, cut your income taxes now, reduce estate tax after your death and benefit a good cause. And, after your death, your family may end up getting just as much as if you hadn't given to the charity. What more could you ask for (from estate planning, at least)?

Charitable trusts are not, of course, for everyone. You've got to make a substantial gift before you get any significant tax benefits. But thanks to the increasingly popular "pooled" trusts, you no longer have to set up your own individual charitable trust, and you can start off by contributing as little as $5,000 to $10,000.

Charitable trusts are quite different from the revocable living trusts that you're probably familiar with. For starters, a charitable trust is not revocable—in other words, once you transfer property to it, that property is gone for good. You cannot change your mind and revoke the trust, regaining legal control of trust property.

Another big difference is that most charitable trusts become operational while you are alive, not at your death. To get the biggest possible tax break, most people create charitable trusts during their highest income-producing years.

There are three main kinds of charitable trusts that may interest you:

- Pooled income trusts, which let you contribute a relatively small amount to a large charitable trust fund.

- Charitable remainder trusts, which you must set up yourself, for larger gifts.
- Charitable lead trusts, which you must also set up yourself, for very large gifts.

1. Pooled Income Trusts

If you don't think that you're a big enough fish, financially, to set up your own charitable trust, check out a pooled income charitable trust. For an initial contribution of about $5,000 to $10,000, you can take advantage of the benefits of charitable trusts. That is, you can take an income tax deduction for your donation, receive income for life and possibly avoid capital gains tax.

You don't set up your own pooled income trust; the charity (or an investment company) does that itself, and then accepts donations from anyone who wishes to contribute. All the donations are pooled in one big fund and then invested, much like a mutual fund. After you make the minimum initial donation, many charities accept subsequent contributions in $1,000 increments.

HOW POOLED INCOME TRUSTS WORK

- You contribute assets to a charity's pooled trust, where your donation is combined with other gifts in one fund.
- You take an income tax deduction, the amount of which is based on the amount of your donation minus the amount you expect to get back as payments from the charity.
- The fund pays income to you (or another "income beneficiary" you name), based on the fund's return on investment.
- You can make additional gifts. If so, you take further income tax deductions and receive correspondingly more income.
- At your death, the assets you contributed go outright to the charity. The value of these assets is not subject to federal estate tax.

Every time you make a donation, you are entitled to take an income tax deduction. You can't deduct the whole amount of your donation; after all, you're getting income back from the charity. The exact amount of your deduction depends on the income beneficiary's life expectancy (in other words, how long he or she is likely to receive income) and the fund's highest yield in the last three years (used to estimate how large the payments will be). (See Section F, below.)

The charity pays income to you (or the income beneficiaries you've named) according to your contribution and the fund's earnings. Commonly, payments are sent quarterly or semiannually. They are taxed as regular income. You can specify that your earnings be retained until you reach a certain age, such as retirement age of 65 or 70, with payments to start then.

After your death, the charity receives your gift outright (and without probate). If the fund was invested wisely, chances are the charity's share of your donation will have significantly appreciated in value by then.

Federal law allows cash contributions or gifts of bonds or stocks, but not tax-exempt ones. You cannot give tangible property—from real estate to jewelry—to a pooled trust. These restrictions do not apply to other types of charitable trusts.

Highly appreciated securities make an excellent gift. That's because the charity can sell them for their present market value and pay no capital gains tax. And because no tax is taken out, more money is left for the charity to invest—which means more income for you.

Example: *Jonathan and his wife Anja are nearing retirement age. They own 500 shares of stock that have gone way up in value—from $20 to $200 per share— but don't produce much in the way of income. They would like to sell the stock and invest the proceeds in income-producing assets, but doing so would mean paying a hefty capital gains tax. They decide, instead, to donate the stock to the pooled charitable trust of the American Foundation for the Blind.*

When they donate the stock, they take a tax deduction for the value of the gift. That amount is calculated by starting with the market value of the stock ($100,000) and subtracting the value of the payments Jonathan and Anja can expect to receive during their lifetimes. The estimate of these payments is based on the pooled fund's recent investment performance and their life expectancies.

The charity takes the stock and sells it. As a tax-exempt charity, it does not owe any capital gains tax on assets that were held at least a year by the donor. Jonathan and Anja's payments from the trust are based on the $100,000 sale proceeds, even though they didn't have to pay taxes on the gain of $180 per share.

One nice feature of pooled trusts is that unlike other charitable remainder trusts, you can keep donating to the trust after you make your initial contribution. So if you don't have a large portfolio or cash to donate at one time, you can still build a good retirement income, and at the same time benefit a good cause, by donating smaller amounts over the years.

Example: *Yuki is in her 40s, with a salary of $80,000 a year. She is not married and has no children. She wants to support her favorite museum and also plan for her retirement. Yuki contributes $10,000 to the museum's charitable pooled fund and takes her income tax deduction, the exact amount of which depends on her life expectancy and the fund's recent performance. A year later, she contributes another $5,000.*

She keeps this up for 20 years, giving more in high-income years and less in years when she has unexpected expenses. By age 65, when she needs the income, her pooled shares, having been well-managed in diversified investments, are worth around $400,000. She will receive the income this amount generates.

Not every charity offers a pooled income trust, but most large ones do. Many universities and museums, for example, have established them. If a pooled fund is available, the charity's "Planned Giving" department will be delighted to discuss it with you and help set up the paperwork. If you like getting information online, you may want to look on the Internet first; many organizations have Web sites that describe their pooled trusts and opportunities for charitable giving.

In a pooled charitable trust, the charity is always the trustee. Its own staff may manage the assets, or the charity may hire a private investment firm to handle them. If you don't think that a charity will manage your gift well, its pooled income charitable trust is not for you.

Pooled charitable trusts must meet strict federal requirements; if they don't, your contributions won't be tax-deductible. (IRC §§ 170(f)(2)(A), 642(c)(5).) The rules dictate who can serve as trustees and how contributions can be combined and invested. If you are dealing with a "brand name" charity's pooled fund, you should be safe. If not, take all the information you can gather about the trust to a good tax advisor before you donate.

CAN'T MAKE UP YOUR MIND?

You can now get the benefits of contributing to a pooled income trust even if you aren't sure what charity you want to benefit. Fidelity Investments, the big mutual fund company, offers a pooled income trust that lets you put off naming a charitable beneficiary as long as you want. The minimum investment is $20,000. For information, call (800) 682-4438.

2. Charitable Remainder Trusts

Typically, only people who want to donate at least $100,000 in cash or securities go to the trouble of creating their own charitable trusts. Most of these trusts are the variety called a charitable remainder trust. With this kind of trust, you create an irrevocable trust to benefit a tax-exempt charity, and then give property to it. The charity manages the trust property and distributes some of the income it produces to you or to someone else you've named. After a certain number of years that you've chosen, or after the income beneficiary dies, the remainder of property goes to the charity outright.

This arrangement offers several benefits:

- An income tax deduction for the value of your gift to the trust (that is, the amount you give minus the amount you expect to get back in the form of income payments.

- Income to you, or someone else you name, for life.

- No capital gains tax to pay if you contribute appreciated property to the trust, leaving more money available for investment.

- Diversification of your investments, because the charity will sell non-income-producing assets and invest them in income-producing ones.

- Tax-free accumulation of earnings, which are taxed only if they are paid out.
- Estate tax savings, because the trust property is not considered part of your estate at your death.
- Probate avoidance, because the assets go directly to the charity, without probate, at your death.

WHY NOT JUST JUMP IN THE POOL?

Pooled income trusts, discussed in the previous section, offer many of the same benefits as do individual charitable remainder trusts—and are considerably cheaper and simpler. So why bother to set up your own charitable trust?

The answer is that although a pooled trust is perfect for many donors, some people want the greater flexibility that a customized trust can provide. For example, a tailor-made trust gives you more control over the amount and frequency of payments the charity makes to you. You can also donate more kinds of property to a private charitable trust; pooled trusts accept only cash and securities.

You can donate almost any kind of property to a charitable remainder trust: real estate, securities, artwork, cash. If the trust property doesn't produce income, the charity will probably sell it and invest the proceeds. If property that's sold has gone up in value since you acquired it, a profit will be made on the sale. If you sold the property yourself, you would owe long-term capital gains tax on that profit. Tax-exempt charities do not, which means that the charity can invest the entire amount.

Example: *Katherine and Grant create a charitable remainder trust and transfer to it stock currently worth $150,000. They bought the stock years ago for $50,000. The charity sells the stock for $150,000 and invests the proceeds for growth and income. No capital gains tax is due, so the whole $150,000 can be* *invested. If Katherine and Grant had sold the stock themselves, they would have owed capital gains tax, leaving less to reinvest.*

The person who receives payments from the trust property is called the income beneficiary. This person—you or someone else you choose—receives a set payment from the trust, or a set percentage of the value of trust property, for a certain period of time. For example, the income beneficiary might receive 7% of the value of the trust each year for life, or a fixed annual sum of $8,000 for life. You cannot give the income beneficiary the right to receive *all* trust income, except in certain situations if the income beneficiary is your spouse.

You state, in the trust document, how long the income beneficiary will receive income from the trust property—a set number of years, or for life. Income beneficiaries never legally own the trust property, and it can never be included in their taxable estates.

The downside to naming someone else to receive payments is that these payments may be subject to gift tax. If an income beneficiary is anyone other than you or your spouse, the payments from the trust are considered a taxable gift from you. Under current rules, if a beneficiary is paid more than $10,000 in a calendar year, you must file a federal gift tax return. You probably won't, however, have to pay any tax in that year. Instead, the amount over $10,000 will count against your personal gift/estate tax exemption. (See Introductory chapter.)

The estate tax break comes when the trust assets become solely owned by the charity—that is, when payments to the income beneficiary come to an end. At that point, the trust property is no longer part of your taxable estate. (If, however, you name someone other than your spouse, and that person survives you, the value of his or her right to receive trust income for life is included in your taxable estate. See Section D.2, below.)

There are two main types of charitable remainder trusts, which differ primarily in the way the income beneficiaries are paid:

- Annuity trusts, which pay the income beneficiary a fixed amount each year.
- Unitrusts, which pay the income beneficiary an amount equal to a percentage of the trust assets each year.

a. Charitable Remainder Annuity Trusts

If you are not concerned about possible inflation eroding the buying power of the income you get from your charitable trust, an annuity trust is often the better choice. This type of trust provides a fixed dollar amount of income every year—an annuity—to the trust's income beneficiary. Whether the trust assets go up or down in value, the payments are always the same. The payments last as long as the beneficiary lives or for a period you name, up to 20 years. (IRC § 664(d).)

Small donors, don't lose heart. *If you're interested in making a charitable donation and securing a fixed income for life, but don't have the big bucks that are necessary to set up your own charitable trust, check out charitable gift annuities. They're discussed in Section E, below.*

Many people name themselves as the income beneficiary and receive the annuity for their lifetime. But you can name someone else, or more than one beneficiary to receive income at the same time. As mentioned, if income goes to anyone but you or your spouse, you may owe gift tax on it. (Choosing beneficiaries is discussed in Section D.2, below.)

In the document that creates the trust, you set the amount of the annuity. The figure is stated as a percentage of the initial value of the assets you transfer to the trust; it must be at least five percent. Once the trust is operational, you can't change that figure. For instance, if you create a trust worth $250,000 and specify that the charity pay you $12,500 a year (the minimum payment) for the rest of your life, you can't later say, "Oops, I forgot about inflation. How about $18,000 a year?" This rule holds true even if the trust assets significantly increase in value, as you hope they will.

The advantage of this type of trust is that if the trust has lower-than-expected income—for example, during a period when interest rates are extremely low—the income beneficiary still receives the same annual income. The trustee must use the trust principal, if necessary, to make the payments. This can't be done with other types of charitable remainder trusts.

The annuity payment can't exceed 50% of the value of the trust. However, the law also requires that the charity actually receive, when the trust ends, at least 10% of the fair market value of the original gift. If the payments are too high, making them will require spending principal, possibly using up much of the gift before the payment term is over. Obviously, this defeats your desire to make a gift to the charity.

There are practical limits, too. First, the higher the payments, the lower your income tax deduction. (See Section F, below.) Second, a charity is unlikely to accept a gift, particularly if it must serve as trustee, if it can't expect to eventually get a significant benefit from it.

After you set up a charitable remainder annuity trust, you cannot give additional assets to it. (Treas. Reg. 1.664-2(b).) Once the trust is created and funded, that's it. Of course, you could create a new, second trust, and many people do, but that's a fair amount of bother. Better to carefully decide, before creating the trust, how much money you want to put in it and how large an annuity you want.

There are also income tax advantages to using an annuity trust instead of a charitable remainder unitrust. That's because property contributed to an annuity trust gets you a bigger income tax deduction than if it were placed in a charitable remainder unitrust. (See Section b, below.)

HOW CHARITABLE REMAINDER ANNUITY TRUSTS WORK

- You fund the trust with, if possible, appreciated assets that aren't producing much income.
- You take an income tax deduction, the amount of which is based on the amount of your donation minus the amount you expect to get back as annuity payments from the charity.
- The trustee (usually, the charity) converts all assets into income-producing ones. No capital gains tax is due on the sale profits.
- The trustee pays a fixed amount to the income beneficiary for the annuity period.
- At the end of the annuity period, trust assets go outright to the charity. The value of these assets is not subject to federal estate tax.

b. Charitable Remainder Unitrusts

This popular form of charitable remainder trust can provide income tax relief, reduce estate tax and provide other benefits. The trustee pays income each year from the trust to an income beneficiary—usually the person who set up the trust. The income beneficiary gets a percentage of the current value of the trust property (or all trust income, in certain circumstances; this is discussed below). For example, the trust document could specify that the income beneficiary receives 7% of the value of the trust assets yearly. (In contrast, the beneficiary of an annuity trust gets the same fixed amount each year.)

Each year, the trust assets must be reappraised to ascertain their current value. If the dollar value of the trust assets increases because of the trustee's wise investment decisions, simple good luck or inflation, the payments received by the income beneficiary also increase. So a charitable remainder unitrust can serve as a hedge against inflation. That's very different from an annuity trust, where payments remain fixed even if inflation runs rampant.

Example: *Felix, age 65, earns a very comfortable salary and owns assets worth $3 million. Much of his property consists of his home and stock that he bought years ago. The stock has appreciated substantially in value; it cost $600,000 and is now worth $1.6 million. It currently pays little in dividends, and when Felix retires, he would like it to yield some income to supplement his Social Security and other retirement income.*

If Felix sells the stock so he can buy income-producing assets, he'll owe capital gains tax on his profit from the sale. Setting up a charitable remainder unitrust offers one way to avoid this tax and guarantee income later, when Felix retires. Felix establishes a charitable remainder trust with himself as the income beneficiary for life and his alma mater, his state's university, as the final charitable beneficiary. Felix gives the stock to the trust.

For income tax purposes, his donation to the charity is the full market value of the stock, reduced by the value of his right to receive the income for life under the terms of the trust. The calculation is based on IRS estimates about Felix's life expectancy and growth of the trust assets. Currently, the income tax deduction would be almost $400,000.

The trustee sells the stock for $1.6 million; the $1 million profit is not taxed. The charity then reinvests the whole amount in profitable investments. The trust document requires income to be paid to Felix at 6% of the trust value annually for life. This figure will be $96,000 the first year; it will change each year as the value of trust assets changes. If the value of the investment increases, Felix will receive more money.

So far, Felix has avoided paying capital gains tax while turning an asset that paid little income into one that pays him much more. With the money he saves because of the income tax deduction, he can buy life insurance to replace the gift amount for his inheritors, if he is healthy. He can then remove the policy proceeds from his taxable estate. (See Section G, below.)

But there is even more good news. Felix has reduced his estate to a level where much less estate tax will be due at his death. Felix has given money to the school for its eventual use instead of giving it to Uncle Sam. And he has a guaranteed income for life.

If Felix lives for 15 years while receiving income from this trust, the trust should pay him at least $96,000 x 15, or $1,440,000. If the trustee invests the original $1.6 million wisely, that principal amount should also increase significantly in 20 years.

As mentioned earlier, the payout rate to the trust income beneficiary must, under IRS rules, be at least 5% and not more than 50%. But practical considerations, such as your desire to make a gift to charity and the charity's willingness to accept and manage the trust property, mandate that the percentage be reasonable. After all, if payments are excessive, they could eat up all the trust property. You must ensure that the charity will eventually receive a significant gift—and the IRS requires that at least 10% of the original assets eventually go to the charity.

If trust income doesn't cover the payments, the general rule is that the trustee must dip into principal. But if the trust is set up as a "net income unitrust," the trustee pays only the income that is earned and leaves the principal untouched. Another option is the net income "with makeup" unitrust. With that variety of trust, if income falls short one year, the trustee can increase payments in future years to make up the difference.

If you name more than one income beneficiary, you don't have to give each one the same percentage. But a beneficiary must receive the same percentage each year.

Example: *Rose and David set up a unitrust, specifying that one of their two grown children should get 8% of the trust's assets each year, and the other 5%. These amounts can't change.*

In certain situations, the trust document can direct that the income beneficiary receive all the income from the trust. This is allowed if:

- your spouse is the income beneficiary, or
- the trust property is your residence or family farm.

If you create a charitable remainder unitrust, you can, later on, transfer more property to the trust, if this power is expressly granted in the original trust document. (Treas. Reg. § 1.664-3(b).)

HOW CHARITABLE REMAINDER UNITRUSTS WORK

- You create and fund the trust, with appreciated assets if possible.
- You take the income tax deduction for the value of your gift, the amount of which is based on the amount of your donation minus the amount you expect to get back as annuity payments from the charity.
- The trustee (usually, the charity) converts all assets into income-producing assets. No capital gains tax is due on any profit from the sales.
- The trustee pays a set percentage of the value of the trust assets—redetermined each year—to the income beneficiary annually.
- At the income beneficiary's death, trust assets go outright to the charity. The value of these assets is not subject to estate tax.

---

3. Charitable Lead Trusts

A charitable lead trust is a rarer form of charitable trust, used mostly by very wealthy people who are worried about high estate taxes. It can be created during your lifetime or, more commonly, at death.

It works like this: When you transfer property to the trust, you must pay estate tax. The trust then makes payments to the charity for a set number of years or your lifetime. Then the property goes back to you or someone you named to inherit it—free (or almost free) of estate tax.

Usually, the final beneficiaries are your spouse or children. In other words, the process is the reverse of that of charitable remainder trusts.

Example: *Sam creates a charitable lead trust that will take effect at his death. When he dies, $1.5 million of his property goes into the trust, which will pay the charity 5% of its value for 10 years. Estate tax is now due on what the IRS tables predict the value of the trust property will be at the end of the 10-year period.*

After 10 years, the trust property goes to Sam's two grown children. The trust principal has by then grown larger than IRS tables predicted it would, but the increase is not subject to estate tax when it passes to Sam's children.

During the years in which the charity is entitled to payments, it is paid an amount guaranteed by the trust document. If the income from the trust property is too little to cover the payments, the charity can dip into the trust principal to make the payments to itself.

The charity may receive either a set percentage of the trust's net worth (that's called a unitrust) each year, or a set dollar amount each year (an annuity trust).

Charitable lead trusts do not offer all the tax advantages of charitable remainder trusts, but they do offer some of the same income tax advantages. For instance, if you donate appreciated property to a charitable lead trust, and the charity then sells it, no capital gains tax is assessed. Also, you can take an income tax deduction of the amount that the charity is expected to receive.

Trusts created at death. A charitable lead trust that takes effect upon your death can help reduce the estate tax bill, give to charity and still (eventually) benefit your family or other beneficiaries. The tax savings come because the value of what the charity will receive as income is not included in your taxable estate.

Example: *Rachel directs in her living trust that upon her death, a charitable lead trust of $1 million be established for a period of 15 years. During those years, annual income payments of $80,000 will go to her favorite charity. After 15 years, the remainder will go to her niece.*

The charity's interest in the trust is calculated using the IRS tables. In this case, it will probably be around $800,000. This $800,000 is deducted from the taxable value of Rachel's estate.

Trusts created during your life. Charitable lead trusts that become operational while you're alive involve a significant income tax drawback: You must pay income tax on the payments made by the trust to the charity during the set payment period. That's because the assets will revert back to you, or your inheritors, later. So you're taxed on income the charity, not you, receives. This can effectively cancel out the original tax deduction—not a desirable state of affairs. Still, if you have highly appreciated assets that you want to remain in the family, the capital gains tax savings these trusts offer can make them a good deal.

Example: *Clark, a wealthy business owner in his early 50s, wants to take advantage of every tax break he can find. He and his wife have many assets that will let them continue to live very well when they retire.*

Clark creates a charitable lead trust, funded with real estate that he long ago paid $200,000 for and which is now worth $2 million. He chooses a research institute investigating Parkinson's disease to receive annual income payments of 8% of the trust assets. At Clark's death, the remaining trust assets are to go to his children.

The trustee sells the real estate and invests the proceeds in mutual funds. Clark avoids the capital gains tax that would have been assessed if he had personally sold the property, because the charity isn't taxed on the sale. Clark takes an immediate income tax deduction of the charity's projected income from these assets, based on the IRS tables that consider interest rates and his life expectancy. He knows he will have to pay tax on the income the charity obtains from these assets, but he hopes the benefit he's achieved from avoiding capital gains tax will more than make up for the loss.

Even more important to him, Clark is able to leave the trust property to his children. Also, he feels satisfaction that he has contributed to valuable research.

It's impossible to say exactly how much income tax Clark will pay on what the trust earns during his life. It depends on how long he lives and on income tax rates. If the value of the trust keeps going up, Clark's tax savings will be eaten away.

HOW CHARITABLE LEAD TRUSTS WORK

- You create and fund the trust, with appreciated assets if possible.
- You take an income tax deduction, the amount of which is based on the amount the charity is expected to receive.
- The trustee converts all trust assets into income-producing assets.
- Income goes to the charity for the period you specify.
- You pay income tax on trust income paid to the charity.
- At the end of the set period, all trust property, including appreciation, goes to the beneficiaries you chose.

D. Setting Up a Charitable Trust

It's undoubtedly obvious that setting up a charitable trust is not a do-it-yourself project. The tax calculations and projections alone can be mind-addling. Fortunately, charities are well-stocked with people who would love nothing more than to discuss your options with you. They may even help in preparing a trust document. Take advantage of their eagerness and their knowledge—but don't rely on them for legal and financial advice. The decisions you must make when setting up a charitable trust are very important, and they are irrevocable.

If you can afford to set up a charitable trust, you can well afford to find a lawyer with plentiful experience in tailoring these trusts to clients' needs. You may also want to talk to a CPA or financial planner about the key issues of how much income you'll need and how much income you can expect the trust assets to produce. These experts should also be able to help you evaluate how the charity will perform in its role as trustee and manager of a big chunk of your money.

1. Selecting a Trustee

If you donate to a pooled income trust, the charity is the trustee. But if you set up your own charitable trust, you'll have to name a trustee.

Most large public charities insist on serving as trustee of any charitable trust from which they benefit. That's fine with most donors, who prefer to turn management and investment responsibilities over to an experienced investment staff. Another advantage is that some charities do not charge anything for acting as trustee—a deal you won't get from a bank or trust company. And the charity, of course, has a strong incentive to make good investments: The bigger the value of the trust, the more the charity gets, eventually.

Especially if you're making a gift to a smaller charity, you may want to do some investigating before accepting the charity as trustee. Its cause may be noble, and its staff dedicated, but that's not a guarantee of sophistication about investments.

First, find out whether or not the charity has a good investment record. An experienced lawyer or CPA can help you. If necessary, your advisor should also be able to suggest other possible trustees, aside from yourself—perhaps a private trust company.

Also look at the charity's management style and the people who will control the trust property. Who in the charity will actually be making investment decisions? Is that person open and easy to talk to? Are you confident in her judgment and human sympathies? How sophisticated are the investment staff's financial knowledge and skills?

2. Choosing Income Beneficiaries

If you donate to a pooled income trust or set up a charitable remainder trust of your own, you must choose income beneficiaries. These are the people who receive payments from the charity before the charity receives the trust assets outright. (With the less common charitable lead trust, the charity is the income beneficiary, and you choose final beneficiaries. See Section C.3, above.)

Most people choose themselves as income beneficiaries, often as a way of locking in some retirement income.

Example: *Len and Hilde are in their early 60's. They donate $100,000 in cash to a charitable remainder unitrust, and name themselves as income beneficiaries for their lives. They set the payout rate at 6% per year. The first year, the trust will pay them $6,000.*

You can, if you wish, name someone else as income beneficiary of a charitable trust. If you name someone other than your spouse, however, there can be estate tax consequences. If the beneficiary survives you, the value of that person's "life interest"—his or her right to receive trust income for life—is included in your taxable estate.

Example: *Quan donates to a pooled income trust and names himself and his daughter as life beneficiaries. When Quan dies, the IRS puts a dollar value on his daughter's right to receive payments for the rest of her life. It includes that amount in Quan's estate for estate tax purposes.*

You don't have to choose just one person to receive the trust payments. If you name more than one income beneficiary, each can receive different amounts. But with an annuity trust, the amount each receives can't change from year to year, and with a unitrust, the percentage each receives can't change.

Example: *Juanita and Adolfo set up a charitable remainder annuity trust, naming their two grown children, Roberto and Francesca, as income beneficiaries. They state, in the trust document, that Roberto is to receive $10,000 each year for life, and that Francesca is to receive $12,000 a year for her life. When Roberto and Francesca have both died, the remaining trust property will belong solely to the charity.*

You can also specify that two or more people receive the payments together.

Example: *Walter, an elderly widower, sets up a charitable remainder unitrust with his daughter and her husband as income beneficiaries. Every year, they will be paid 8% of the value of the trust assets. When one of them dies, the survivor will receive the whole payment each year, for the rest of his or her life.*

3. Controlling Where Your Money Ends Up

Most charities allow you to designate, with some specificity, the ultimate recipient of your gift. For example, you could name the biology department of a university or a hospital program for children. This is true even with a pooled income trust, where your contribution is mixed with those of other donors.

COMPARING TYPES OF CHARITABLE TRUSTS

	Pooled Income Trust	Charitable Remainder	Charitable Remainder Annuity Trust	Charitable Lead Trust
Primary goals	Income tax and estate tax savings; income, possibly for retirement	Income tax and estate tax savings; fixed income for life	Income tax and estate tax savings; hedge against inflation	Income tax and estate tax savings (though can cause significant tax disadvantages); preservation of trust assets for final beneficiaries
Property you can transfer	Money or stocks	Money or tangible property	Money or tangible property	Money or tangible property
Transfer additional property later	Yes	No	Yes	Yes, if permitted in original trust document
Your income tax deduction available to you	Yes	Larger than with unitrust, because IRS values charity's share higher	Smaller than with annuity trust, because IRS values charity's share as less	The value of charity's income interest for set period
Trustee	The charity	Anyone you choose, including yourself or the charity	Anyone you choose, including yourself or the charity	Anyone you choose, including yourself or the charity
Income beneficiary	You or anyone else you name	You or anyone else you name	You or anyone else you name	The charity
Final beneficiary	The charity	The charity	The charity	You or anyone else you name
Income paid to income beneficiary	Interest earned from donor's contribution to the pool	Fixed dollar amount each year, even if trust principal must be used. Must be minimum of 5% of initial fair market value of trust assets	Fixed percentage of trust assets each year	Fixed dollar or percentage of trust assets, whichever you specify in trust document

E. Charitable Gift Annuities

Another way to get the benefits of a charitable trust, without contributing tens of thousands of dollars to a charity, is to buy what's called a charitable gift annuity. Many charities—from big universities, performing arts centers and hospitals to small churches and community colleges—now offer them.

By transferring a relatively small amount of money to the charity, you get an immediate income tax deduction, fixed payments for life and eventual estate tax savings. The charity benefits from your generosity after your death, when it receives outright the amount you gave—increased, it hopes, by investment over the years. Exactly how much it receives depends on how long you live and how well the original gift was invested.

1. How Charitable Gift Annuities Work

To set up a charitable gift annuity, you transfer cash, securities or (if state law allows) real estate to a charity. Many charities require a minimum of only a few thousand dollars. Part of what you transfer is simply a charitable gift, and part goes for the purchase of an annuity contract. Under that contract, the charity agrees to pay you an annuity—a set amount every year—for your life, and for the life of another beneficiary ("annuitant") if you've named one. To ensure that the guaranteed payments will be made, the charity contracts with a private annuity company.

Amount of payments. The annual amount the annuitant receives is a percentage of the amount you transfer to the charity. The percentage depends on the annuitants' age: The older they are, the larger the payments. (Standard rates of return are listed in the table below.)

Taxation of payments. A certain portion of the payments is taxable as ordinary income; the rest is tax-free. That's because payments represent both interest and a return of principal, and the return of principal isn't taxed. The split depends on how many annuitants there are, and how old they are. Payments are not counted as income when it comes to determining Social Security payments.

Income tax deduction. You also get an immediate income tax deduction for your charitable gift. The amount of the deduction depends on the IRS's estimate of the value of your gift. That, in turn, depends on current interest rates, which change monthly.

After the death of the annuitants, your gift goes to the charity.

Example: *Isaac and Amelia, both in their mid-70s, decide to establish a charitable gift annuity with CARE, a charity that helps needy people around the world. CARE requires a $3,000 minimum gift. Isaac and Amelia give $10,000. Their rate of return, based on their ages, is 7.5%, which means they will receive $750 a year for the rest of their lives. They decide to receive payments quarterly. After one dies, the other will keep on receiving the same amount for life.*

Under IRS tables (recalculated every month), they can take a $3,622 income tax deduction in the year they make the gift. And based on their life expectancies, $370 of each annuity payment is tax-free.

GIFT ANNUITY RATES AND INCOME TAX DEDUCTIONS

(suggested by American Council on Gift Annuities)

One Life			Two Lives		
Age	Rate of Return	Approximate Charitable Deduction (amount given to charity)	Age	Rate of Return	Approximate Charitable Deduction (amount given to charity)
50	6.5%	31%	50, 50	6.3%	26%
55	6.7	33	55, 55	6.5	27
60	6.9	36	60, 60	6.6	29
65	7.2	40	65, 65	6.8	32
70	7.7	42	70, 70	7.1	35
75	8.4	46	75, 75	7.5	39
80	9.4	50	80, 80	8.2	43
85	10.5	55	85, 85	9.2	47

2. Kinds of Property to Transfer

You can always use cash or securities to buy a charitable gift annuity. Some states also allow you to use real estate. Some people donate their homes, with the proviso that they have the right to live there for the rest of their lives. If you transfer real estate, the charity will have to sell it to get income-producing assets; the amount of your donation will be decreased by the costs of sale.

As with other kinds of charitable gifts, you get an extra benefit from donating property that has gone up in value since you acquired it. You will owe no capital gains tax on the portion of the property that is considered a gift to the charity. You will owe capital gains tax on the rest of the amount, which is being used to buy the annuity contract. But if you are both the donor and the annuitant, you can spread out payments for the capital gains tax over your life expectancy.

3. When Payments Start

If you don't need annuity payments right now, but would like to start making charitable gifts, you can buy what's called a deferred-payment annuity. You can take the tax deduction for your donation now, but you put off receiving the annuity payments until you're older—say, 65 and retired, probably in a lower income tax bracket. With a deferred-payment annuity, your payments will be higher once they start, and more of each payment will be tax-free.

4. Choosing Beneficiaries: Tax Consequences

An annuity contract can have one or two beneficiaries (annuitants). Whom you choose to receive annuity income will have a big effect on both income tax and gift tax.

Just You. If you make the charitable gift and are the sole annuitant, you pay income tax on only part of each payment; often, more than half of the payment is tax-free. That's because part of that money is seen as a tax-free return of your principal, and the rest as ordinary, taxable income. Each year, the charity will send you an IRS Form 1099-R, stating how much of your annuity income is taxable. If you live beyond your statistical life expectancy, the entire payment is taxed as ordinary income.

Just Someone Else. The beneficiary must pay income tax on the annuity payments, just like ordinary income. You will also be assessed gift tax on the amount the other person receives. If it's greater than $10,000 per year, you'll have to file a federal gift tax return.

You and Your Spouse. If you transfer your own assets to the charity, but name your spouse as an annuitant along with you, your spouse will have to pay regular income tax on her share of the annuity payments. You will not be assessed gift tax, because gifts to spouses are gift tax-free.

You and Someone Else During Your Life. If you name someone else, not your spouse, to receive income for as long as you yourself live, this other beneficiary must pay income tax on the annuity payments, just like ordinary income. You will also be assessed gift tax on the amount the other person receives. If it's greater than $10,000 per year, you'll have to file a federal gift tax return.

You During Your Life, and Then Someone Else. If you wish, you can receive annuity income during your life, and designate another beneficiary to receive payments for his or her life after your death. The recipient will have to pay income tax on the payments as ordinary income.

There's a gift/estate tax complication here. Because you're giving the beneficiary a "future interest"—that is, he or she isn't getting anything now—it doesn't qualify for the annual $10,000/recipient exclusion from federal gift tax. You can get around this problem by adding some language to the annuity contract. The contract should contain a clause stating that you reserve the right to revoke, in your will, the beneficiary's interest. Presto, no gift has been made at all, so no gift tax applies. The gift will be made at your death, which means that the value of the beneficiary's interest will be included in your taxable estate.

Example: *Eloise sets up a charitable gift annuity with her alma mater, the state university. With an eye toward setting up some guaranteed retirement income, she names herself as the annuitant for her lifetime. After her death, she wants payments to go to her son Ben. In the annuity contract, she inserts a clause reserving the right to revoke Ben's right to the annuity. At Eloise's death, the value of the annuity is included in her taxable estate.*

5. Putting Conditions on Use of Your Charitable Gift

Charitable organizations prefer gifts with no strings attached. That way, they can decide, when they actually are free to use the money, where it's most needed. You can, however, usually specify how you want your gift used. For example, you might endow a position at a university, set up a scholarship fund or earmark the funds for research on a problem that's important to you. Your wishes should be set out in the annuity contract.

F. The Income Tax Deduction for Charitable Gifts

Whether you create a charitable trust or make an outright gift, you may get substantial income tax advantages from giving to a charity. That's because you can deduct the value of the gift to the charity (as determined by the IRS) from your income tax.

1. Amount of the Deduction

If you just write a check to a charity, without using a trust, you can simply deduct the amount of the gift on your next income tax return. (If the gift is very large, you'll probably have to take the deduction over several years; see Section 2, below.)

It's not so simple, however, with a charitable trust or charitable gift annuity. Where things get tricky is in determining the actual value of the gift for income tax deduction purposes. The value is not just the value of the property when you give it to the trust. After all, with a charitable remainder trust or charitable gift annuity, you (or someone else you've named) will get payments back from the charity. And with a charitable lead trust, you or your heirs will eventually get the trust property itself back.

Here's how the IRS figures it out. With a charitable remainder trust, the IRS starts with the value of the property. Then it deducts the estimated value of the income beneficiary's right to receive payments from the trust property. This estimate is based on the income beneficiary's life expectancy and the expected return from investment of the charitable gift property. These factors are taken into account by using tables published by the IRS. The charity you give to, or an accountant or lawyer, can help you figure out the exact numbers for your situation.

Example: *Barbara and Frank, a couple in their 60s, give stock worth $25,000 to the pooled income trust of their favorite charity. They will receive payments for life from the trust. Based on their life expectancies and the pooled income fund's recent performance, they are entitled to an income tax deduction of approximately $7,500.*

With a charitable lead trust, things are reversed. The income tax deduction is the estimated value of the income the charity will receive.

2. When You Can Take the Deduction

Once you know the worth of a gift to a charity, under IRS rules you are entitled to deduct 100% of this amount. But if the gift is very large relative to your current income, you can't take the deduction in a single year. Instead, it must be spread out over up to six years.

The IRS limits the size of the charitable deduction you can take in a single year, whether or not your gift was made using a trust. The most you can possibly deduct in one year is 50% of your adjusted gross income. The actual limit that applies in your situation depends on:

- how the IRS classifies the charity
- your annual income, and
- what kind of property you give to the charity.

The charity's classification. To qualify for the 50% limit, the recipients of your gifts must be classified by the IRS as "public" charities. Most widely known charities meet this requirement, such as schools, churches, the Salvation Army, the American Cancer Society and most environmental organizations.

Many private foundations, however, are not public charities. If your gift is made to one of them, the most you can deduct the first year is 30% of your adjusted gross income. You can deduct the rest over the next five years. To determine whether you are eligible for the 50% or 30% deduction, check the IRS's list of charities in IRS Publication 78, or look at the list online at www.irs.gov/prod/search/eosearch.html.

Example 1: *Christopher creates a charitable remainder trust, with the public charity CARE as the final beneficiary. He names himself as the income beneficiary. The IRS will determine the worth of his gift, for income tax purposes, by subtracting the value of his retained interest in the income from the value of the trust principal. The result is less than 50% of his income for the year, so he may deduct the entire gift that year.*

Example 2: *Marlys makes a large gift to a tax-exempt family foundation that is not in the IRS 50% category. She can claim a charitable deduction for no more than 30% of the amount of her adjusted gross income on that year's tax return. She has five more years in which she can claim the rest of her deduction.*

The limit on charitable deductions applies to your total charitable deductions for the year. You must take into account all your charitable donations, to all organizations, when you calculate your maximum allowable deduction.

Example: *Beth makes large cash gifts to the National Audubon Society and the University of Michigan, and some smaller gifts to local charities. All the charities are public charities in the eyes of the IRS. These gifts total $25,000— more than half of Beth's $40,000 adjusted gross income for the year. She can deduct $20,000 this year, and carry over the remaining $5,000 deduction to next year's tax return.*

G. Replacing Donated Money for Your Family

One concern of nearly everyone who gives substantial amounts to charity is that by giving away that property, they may be shortchanging their own family. What can you do if you would like to donate large sums to charity, but are afraid that surviving family members might need the money?

There is good news. The tax savings you can realize from charitable gifts may make it possible for you to replace the money given to the charity—a true win-win situation.

For example, you are in luck if you are in good health. Many people take the money they save by virtue of a big charitable income tax deduction and buy life insurance to cover the money "lost" by the gift to the charity. You can then remove the life insurance from your estate for estate tax purposes by giving the policy to the beneficiary or to a life insurance trust. (See Chapter 7.)

Another strategy is available if you give appreciated securities to a charity. Using the money you save in taxes, you can buy the same securities on the open market, at their now higher price. You'll still have the same investment portfolio, but a higher cost basis. (Cost basis is discussed in Chapter ___.) So if you eventually sell the securities, or give them to family members, much less capital gains tax will be due.

∎

CHAPTER 7

Transfer Ownership of Your Life Insurance Policies

When people sit down to make a rough estimate of their net worth to see whether or not they should even worry about estate taxes, they usually tote up all their big assets: house, car, savings and so on. What they may overlook are life insurance proceeds that will be paid after their death. That's a mistake. That money is part of your estate and is subject to estate tax, says the IRS. Several hundred thousand dollars worth of life insurance proceeds can, obviously, create estate tax liability where none existed before.

With a little planning, however, you can avoid taxation of life insurance proceeds. Whether or not life insurance proceeds are included in your taxable estate depends on who owns the policy at your death. If you own the policy, the full amount of the proceeds is included in your federal taxable estate. But if someone else owns it, the proceeds are not included.

Example: *Melissa buys an insurance policy covering her life, with a face value of $200,000. Her son, Jeff, is the beneficiary. Melissa's business partner, Juanita, owns a second policy covering Melissa's life for $400,000, payable to Juanita. Juanita plans to use the proceeds to buy out Jeff, who will inherit Melissa's half of the business, after Melissa's death.*

When Melissa dies, the proceeds of her policy, $200,000, are included in her federal taxable estate. However, none of the $400,000 from the policy Juanita owns is part of Melissa's taxable estate, because Melissa did not own the policy.

There are two ways you can transfer ownership of a life insurance policy, and so get it out of your estate:

- Give the policy to another person.
- Create an irrevocable life insurance trust, and give the policy to the trust.

This chapter discusses both strategies.

A. Giving a Policy to Another Person

You have the right to give ownership of ("assign") your life insurance policy to any other adult, including the policy beneficiary. The only exceptions are some group policies, in which many people participate through work, which don't allow you to transfer ownership. Transferring a life insurance policy must, however, be done with the knowledge of, and with forms approved by, the issuing company. The transfer won't be legally effective if the insurance company has no record of it.

1. Once It's Gone, It's Gone

Transferring ownership of your policy to someone else involves a trade-off: Once the policy is transferred, you've lost all your power over it, forever. You cannot cancel it or change the beneficiary, things you could do if you kept ownership. For example, suppose you transfer ownership of your policy to your spouse, and later get divorced. You cannot cancel the policy or recover it from your ex.

If you keep any of what lawyers call the "incidents of ownership" of a life insurance policy, the IRS considers you the owner. The term "incidents of ownership" simply means any significant power over the policy. Specifically, the proceeds of the policy will be included in your taxable estate if you have the legal right to do any of the following:

- change or name beneficiaries of the policy
- borrow against the policy, pledge any cash reserve it has or cash it in
- surrender, convert or cancel the policy
- select a payment option—that is, decide whether payments to the beneficiary will be in a lump sum or in installments.

2. The Three-Year Requirement

The IRS has some special rules about giving away a life insurance policy. One of the most important is that you must make the gift at least three years before your death. If you don't, the IRS will consider you the owner, for federal estate tax purposes. This means that the full amount of the proceeds is included in your estate, just as if you had kept the policy.

Example: *Louise gives her life insurance policy, with proceeds of $300,000, to her friend Leon. She dies two years later. For federal estate tax purposes, the gift is "disallowed," and all the proceeds, $300,000, are included in Louise's taxable estate. If Louise had transferred the policy more than three years before her death, none of the proceeds would have been included in her taxable estate.*

The message here is obvious: If you want to give away a life insurance policy to reduce estate taxes, do it as soon as you reasonably can. (And don't die for at least three years.)

3. Future Premium Payments

After the policy is transferred, the new owner should make all premium payments, unless of course the policy is fully paid for. If you keep making payments, the IRS might contend, after your death, that you kept an "incident of ownership," and include the proceeds of the policy in your estate—precisely what you're trying to avoid. If the new owner can't afford to pay the premiums, you can give her money for the payments.

To sidestep the issue of future premium payments, consider buying the whole policy outright before you give it away. With such a policy, called a single-premium policy, there's no question about who makes future payments; there aren't any. However, there can be a drawback here, too. A paid-up policy is worth more, for gift tax purposes, than one with premiums left to pay. The value of the policy, at the time of the gift, may exceed the amount that can be given free of federal gift tax, which is currently $10,000 per year per recipient. If so, gift tax will be assessed on all value over the tax-exempt amount. By contrast, if you give a policy that isn't subject to gift tax, every year you can give the new owner no more than the gift tax-exempt amount to pay for annual premiums. As long as the annual premiums don't exceept the exempt amount, no gift tax will be assessed.

4. Gift Tax Issues

When you give away a life insurance policy, the transaction is subject to federal gift tax. Under current law, if the policy has a present value of more than $10,000 and is transferred to one person, gift tax will be assessed. (Gift tax is discussed in detail in Chapter 1.)

You may wonder, given that gift tax and estate tax rates are the same, why there is a tax advantage to giving the policy away now instead of leaving it later. The answer is that for gift tax purposes, the amount taxed is the *present value* of the policy. But if you own the policy at your death, the value of the *proceeds*—a much larger amount—is subject to estate tax.

Example: *Eugene buys a $300,000 universal life insurance policy and gives it to his son, David. Under IRS rules, the value of the policy when he transfers it is $22,000. Because $12,000 of this value is subject to gift tax, Eugene has used up $12,000 of his personal gift/estate tax exemption. Eugene dies ten years later, and David collects the $300,000. None of this $300,000 is included in Eugene's federal taxable estate.*

How much is a life insurance policy worth for gift tax purposes? Under IRS rules, the value is its current cost (what it would cost to buy a similar policy now), not the cash surrender value (what you could get from the insurance company if you canceled the policy). For fully paid-for policies, this value is easy to determine, but if further payments will be made, the value of the gift is harder to figure out. Fortunately, your insurance company can crunch the numbers and tell you the dollar value, for gift tax purposes, of your policy.

Most insurance companies will provide, on request, an informal estimate of the gift tax value of a policy before you make the actual gift. They will also give you the forms (usually, Treasury Department Form 938) that you must submit with your gift tax return, if need be.

5. How to Transfer Ownership of Your Policy

You can give away ownership of your life insurance policy by signing a simple document, called an "assignment" or a "transfer." To do this, notify the insurance company and use its transfer form. There's normally no charge to make the change.

B. Setting Up a Life Insurance Trust

Another way to remove life insurance proceeds from your estate is to set up an irrevocable life insurance trust. After doing the paperwork to create the trust, you transfer your life insurance policy to it. Because the policy is now owned by this legally independent trust, you are not the owner of the insurance proceeds, and they are not included in your taxable estate. The beneficiaries of the policy remain the same as they were before you set up the trust.

Why create a life insurance trust, rather than just transfer a life insurance policy to someone else? The truth is that for most people, simply giving the policy to someone is a better approach. But perhaps there's no one you want to own your policy. For example, perhaps you would like to give an insurance policy on your life to one of your grown offspring, but you aren't confident that she would always pay the policy premiums. With a trust, you can specify that the policy must be kept in effect while you live, eliminating the risk that a new owner of the policy could cash it in.

Example: *Marcie is the divorced mother of two children, in their 20s, who are the beneficiaries of her life insurance policy. Neither is yet a trustworthy money manager. Marcie has an estate of $600,000, plus universal life insurance that will pay $500,000 at her death. She would like to get the policy proceeds out of her taxable estate, but there's no one she trusts enough to own her policy outright. She's afraid that her kids might not make the premium payments, or might even cash in the policy in a time of financial desperation.*

She decides to appoint her sister, the person she's closest to, to be the trustee of a life insurance trust for the policy. She creates a trust and transfers ownership of the life insurance policy to it. After Marcie's death, her sister will handle the money for the children under the terms of the trust document.

See a lawyer first. *If you want to explore using a life insurance trust, see an experienced lawyer before you trundle off to your insurance company. In addition to the complexities of any irrevocable trust, there are also problems unique to a life insurance trust.*

1. IRS Requirements

Strict IRS requirements govern irrevocable life insurance trusts. To gain the estate tax savings you're after, you must conform to these rules.

IRS RULES FOR TAX-SAVING LIFE INSURANCE TRUSTS

- The trust must be irrevocable.
- You cannot be the trustee.
- You must establish the trust at least three years before your death.

a. Only Irrevocable Trusts Allowed

The life insurance trust must be absolutely irrevocable. If you retain any right to revoke or amend the trust or affect the insurance policy in any way (such as naming a new beneficiary), the IRS will consider you to be the legal owner of the policy. That means the proceeds will be included in your taxable estate.

b. Trustee Restrictions

Because the IRS says you cannot control the trust, it follows that you cannot be the trustee. If you try to retain any of the rights that a trustee must have, the IRS will say you still own the policy—and tax the proceeds at your death.

The trustee will have as much power as you grant him or her in the trust document. The trustee commonly has the authority to change the beneficiaries.

Your spouse can be trustee, but you must be careful with this arrangement. You'll need expert legal help to make sure that your spouse is not given powers that might make him or her the legal owner of the policy. After all, you want to keep the proceeds out of both of your estates, not just your own.

You can name your grown child, a sibling, a friend or, if all else fails, an institution such as a bank or trust company to serve as trustee. (It can be tough, however, to find an institution willing to serve as trustee at all, let alone for a reasonable fee.) No matter whom you choose, you'll have more influence over the trustee than you would over someone to whom you gave an insurance policy outright. That's because you create the trust document that establishes the trustee's powers.

c. The Three-Year Requirement

The trust must own the insurance policy for at least three years before your death. If it hasn't, the IRS disregards the trust for estate tax purposes, and the insurance proceeds are included in your taxable estate. (IRC § 2042.)

Obviously, this three-year rule is crucial. It means that if you want to establish an irrevocable life insurance trust, do it now—there are no benefits from waiting. If you miss the three-year requirement, your family won't get any estate tax savings, and you'll have wasted and time and money spent setting up the trust.

The reason for this three-year rule is that the estate tax savings offered by an irrevocable life insurance trust (or any transfer of life insurance ownership) can be so substantial that the IRS wants to prohibit last-minute transfers of life insurance made in anticipation of death. Three years seems like a pretty long last minute, but sensible or not, that's the rule.

2. Future Premium Payments

If you create an irrevocable life insurance trust, you'll have to figure out how future premium payments will be made. Several options are available to you.

a. Single-Premium Policies

With a single-premium policy, there's no worry about future payments. Before you transfer the policy to the trust, you pay, up-front, all premiums due for the duration of the policy.

Normally, any policy with a savings feature (that is, anything but term insurance) can be purchased with a single premium. Obviously, this requires coming up with a large amount of cash—$5,000, $10,000 or much more, depending on your age and the amount of the policy.

b. Giving Money to the Trust

A method that has the virtue of simplicity is to give money to the trust every year, and have the trustee use it to pay the premiums. Gifts to a trust, however, are not eligible for the $10,000 annual gift tax exclusion. So you will have to file a gift tax return for any money you give to the trust.

c. Giving Money to the Beneficiaries

If you trust the beneficiaries, you can give them money each year so that they can make the premium payments on behalf of the trust. If you give anyone more than $10,000 in a calendar year, however, you'll have to file a federal gift tax return.

d. "Crummey" Trust Provisions

You can include what are called "Crummey" provisions (so named because someone named Crummey was the first to have this type of trust validated) in the document that creates your irrevocable life insurance trust. This lets you give money for payment of insurance premiums and use the $10,000 annual gift tax exemption.

Here's how Crummey trust provisions work. The trust document states that each year, each trust beneficiary has the right to receive up to $10,000 from the trust property. (That, remember, is currently the maximum that can be given to a beneficiary, per year, free of gift tax.) Usually the beneficiaries are given a deadline, say January 15, to claim their money for the year.

Each year, you give as much money as is needed to pay the policy premiums—up to $10,000 per beneficiary—to the trust. Now things get tricky. Each year the beneficiaries decline to accept this money. By doing this, the gift is converted from a "future interest" (not eligible for the annual gift tax exemption) into a gift of a "present interest"—which means it qualifies for this exemption. The trustee uses this money to pay that year's insurance premium. If any money is left over after the year's premiums have been paid, it is saved in the trust for future premium payments.

⚠ **The Crummey strategy may soon disappear.** *In 1998, President Clinton proposed legislation that would eliminate the Crummey strategy. (IRC § 2523(c) would be amended.) If Crummey provisions are outlawed, gifts using this method will be taxable and won't qualify for the annual exemption. Even so, gift tax on the amount of premiums is small when compared to the eventual proceeds.*

3. Tailoring Your Trust to Your Needs

Tricky personal concerns can arise when you use an irrevocable life insurance trust. You can't anticipate everything, of course, but you should try to tailor trust provisions to your circumstances as much as you can. There is no standard, one-size-fits-all life insurance trust. And remember, this trust is irrevocable—you've got to get it right the first time.

One big issue to think about, and discuss with an experienced lawyer, is that of beneficiaries. Once a trust owns a policy, your hands are tied when it comes to changing the beneficiaries. What if you get married or have a child after setting up an irrevocable trust? Legally, it's up to the trustee to decide who the beneficiaries of the policy should be. Of course, a trustee who cares for you will probably revise the insurance beneficiaries as you want. For example, the trustee could add your new child as a beneficiary. Obviously, you want to name a trustee who will understand and carry out your wishes.

Or suppose you get divorced, and your ex-spouse is one of the beneficiaries of the life insurance policy and also of Crummey trust provisions you created to pay the premiums. Here's where matters can get very touchy. If the trustee simply removes the ex-spouse as a beneficiary of the policy, the ex-spouse could claim the trustee was really acting under your control. This could cause the entire trust to fail for estate tax purposes.

DO YOU NEED LIFE INSURANCE?

Americans hold an estimated two trillion dollars worth of life insurance—far more, per capita, than any other country, and much of it unnecessary. If you're considering shelling out big bucks for life insurance, here are some factors to consider.

Short-Term Needs

- How much quick cash will family members need to pay debts, funeral expenses and taxes? Federal estate taxes aren't due until nine months after death.
- Will most of your assets be tied up in probate? If you avoid probate's delays by leaving some money and securities in joint or pay-on-death accounts or in joint tenancy, there's usually little need for insurance for short-term expenses.
- How much of your assets are liquid—that is, can quickly be converted to cash? If your estate holds money in bank accounts and marketable securities, there should be plenty of cash. If major assets are hard to sell—for example, real estate or small business interests—then life insurance can provide ready cash so that a forced and perhaps unprofitable sale won't be necessary.
- If you are sole owner of a business and expect your inheritors to continue it, how much cash would it need on your death? If you don't expect your inheritors to continue the business, they'll need only enough cash to keep the business alive until it is sold.

Long-Term Needs

- How many people really depend on your earning capacity over the long term?
- How much money would your dependents need, and for how long, if you died suddenly? How much would they get from Social Security and any private insurance plans that cover you, such as union or management pensions or a group life insurance plan?
- Will dependents have other sources of income, such as scholarships or help from grandparents? Remember that spouses caring for young children usually return to work at some point; they don't need to be supported forever.

C. Types of Life Insurance to Give

For estate planning purposes, there are two main types of life insurance: term, which provides insurance only for a set period, and "permanent" insurance, which you have the right to renew as long as you live.

If you want to give away an insurance policy, choose the permanent variety. Permanent insurance includes whole life, universal life and variable life (discussed below). Any of these types of life insurance can be purchased with one lump sum, called a "single-premium payment." As discussed above (Section B.2), paying for a policy now means you don't have to worry about who makes the premium payments after you give ownership of the policy to a trust or another person.

HOW SAFE IS YOUR INSURANCE COMPANY?

As some surprised and angry policy owners have learned, badly managed insurance companies can go broke. A few insurance companies invested heavily in junk bonds and shaky real estate deals during the '80s, and paid the price when glimmers of fiscal sanity returned to these areas in the '90s.

There is no national or federal insurance guarantee fund for life insurance companies similar to FDIC insurance for bank depositors. In 47 states, there is some sort of industry-sponsored state guarantee fund. (Colorado, Louisiana, New Jersey and the District of Columbia have no such funds.) Although these guarantee funds mean you probably won't lose everything you invested if your insurer goes broke, you certainly don't want to have to wait for state regulators to take charge of an insolvent company and finally—and it can take a while—determine how much money you get back.

To avoid this sad scenario, check the financial stability of the insurer you plan to buy from against one—or even better, two—of these rating systems:

- Weiss Research (the most rigorous of the bunch)
- A.M. Best (Best Insurance Reports) (www.ambest.com)
- Duff & Phelps
- Moody's Investors Service
- Standard and Poor's
- Comdex (a composite rating based on the Duff & Phelps, Moody's, Standard and Poor's and A.M. Best ratings).

You should be able to locate the reports of these companies at a large public library or online. Or ask your insurance agent for help. These online sites may be helpful:

- The Insurance News Network, www.insure.com/ratings, shows ratings from Standard and Poor's and Duff & Phelps.
- Northwood/Roche, www.northwoodroche.com, a California discount insurance broker, will e-mail you free ratings from any of the big ratings services.

1. Term Insurance

Term insurance provides a set amount of cash if you die while the policy is in force. For example, a five-year term policy pays off if you die within five years—and that's it. If you live beyond the end of the term, you get nothing (except, of course, the continued joys and sorrows of life itself). The policy does not develop reserves.

Term insurance is the cheapest form of coverage, particularly suitable for younger people with families. The older you are, the more expensive term insurance becomes.

It rarely makes sense to give away a term life insurance policy in an effort to avoid estate tax. Although some term policies are automatically renewable at the end of the term without a medical examination (often for higher premiums), you never lock in the right to maintain the policy no matter how old you become.

2. Permanent Insurance

If you own a permanent insurance policy—that is, one you can automatically renew for as long as you live—it's a good idea to consider giving it away to avoid having the proceeds taxed at your death.

With a permanent policy, premium payments for the first few (or more) years cover more than the company's cost (based on the actuarial risk of death) to cover you. The excess money goes into a reserve account, which the insurance company invests. Unless the company is disastrously managed, these investments yield returns—interest or dividends. Some of this money is passed along to you. It can be added to your policy reserves or you can borrow against it, after a set time. And if you decide to end the policy, you can cash it in for the "surrender value."

Returns that accumulate are not taxable unless the money is actually distributed to you. Certain partial withdrawals can even be made without paying tax.

There are three primary kinds of permanent insurance: whole life, universal life and variable life.

a. Whole Life Insurance

Whole life (sometimes called "straight life") insurance provides a set dollar amount of coverage that can never be canceled, in exchange for fixed, uniform payments. Because the payments are the same throughout your life, the premiums are comparatively high (versus your statistical risk of death) in the early years of the policy. This is why reserves are built up. If you live a long while after the policy is issued, your payments become low, compared to your risk of death.

b. Universal Life Insurance

Universal life combines some of the desirable features of term and whole life insurance. You build up a cash reserve, as with whole life. Like term insurance, you can vary premium payments, the amount of coverage or both, from year to year. Over time, the net cost usually is lower than whole life insurance. Also, you'll probably get more information than you would if you bought a whole life policy. For example, the company will disclose how much of your premiums will go for company overhead, reserves and policy proceed payments, and how much will be kept for your savings.

c. Variable Life Insurance

Variable life, sometimes called "variable universal life insurance," refers to policies in which cash reserves are invested in stocks and bonds. In a sense, these policies combine insurance with a mutual fund. Because over the past decade overall prices on the stock market have risen dramatically, variable life policies have usually produced the best returns. But of course, these policies are almost sure to fare less well when financial markets decline.

d. Cash to Pay Estate Tax: Survivorship Life Insurance

If you are married and expect substantial estate tax to be owed when the second spouse dies, you may want to consider a relatively new type of insurance called survivorship life insurance, also known as "second to die" or "joint" insurance. It is commonly used to provide cash to pay estate tax, and is particularly useful when your major assets aren't liquid—for example, a business or real estate.

A survivorship policy insures two lives, usually spouses. When the first spouse dies, no proceeds are paid. The policy remains in force, and premiums must continue to be paid, until the second spouse dies. The policy then pays off.

Because two lives are insured, premiums for survivorship life policies are comparatively low compared to policies on each person's life. Of course, cost also depends on your age and health.

Gifts of survivorship life insurance. *Because this kind of policy involves new and complex tax issues, check with a good estate planning lawyer if you want to give one away. It may be best to have the policy owned by a life insurance trust.*

BUYING INSURANCE

Before you contact anyone who sells insurance, you should have a good idea of what kind of policy you need and how much it should cost. The cost of the same insurance can vary considerably from company to company. Often, relatively small companies charge lower rates than some of the giants of TV advertising, and some brokers charge discount commissions.

Some books that may be helpful include:

- *How to Insure Your Life*, by Reg Wilson & the Merritt Editors (Merritt)
- *Your Life Insurance Options*, by Alan Lavine (John Wiley and Sons, Inc.)

You can also contact a free life insurance rate-shopping service, which will provide information on the costs of different companies' policies. These resources include:

- Select Quote, 800-289-5807, www.selectquote.com
- Insurance Quote, 800-972-1104, www.thirdstreet.com/iquote/index.htm
- Quotesmith, 800-556-9393, www.quotesmith.com

If you're ready to buy, talk to an insurance salesperson or broker. Normally, a salesperson sells for one company only, while a broker can place your policy with one of several. In theory, this would seem to be a reason to prefer a broker, but in practice, the integrity of the person you are dealing with is the most important factor.

Look for a person who will function as an ally, offering information and proposing alternatives. If you get quick-sell pressure, look elsewhere. And here's one more tip: Some salespeople don't recommend that you buy term insurance, or try to talk you out of it, for no other reason than that they get a much higher commission from selling you whole life or universal.

D. Choosing Life Insurance Beneficiaries

As you know, when you buy life insurance, you name the policy's beneficiaries—those who will receive the proceeds when you die. As long as you own the policy, you can change beneficiaries. Once you transfer ownership to someone else or to a trust, however, you can no longer change your mind about beneficiaries.

To change a beneficiary, contact your insurance agent or company, and complete the form provided by the insurer. You cannot make this change in your will or living trust. A will or living trust has no effect on who gets the proceeds of an insurance policy.

> **INCOME TAXATION OF INSURANCE PROCEEDS**
>
> Cash policy proceeds paid to a beneficiary after an insured's death are exempt from federal income taxes, and from state income tax in most states. If, however, the proceeds are paid in installments, any interest paid on the principal is taxable income to the recipient.

1. Special Rules for Community Property States

If you live in a community property state and buy a policy with community property funds, one-half of the proceeds will be owned by the surviving spouse—no matter who the policy names as the beneficiary. If you want only one spouse to control who gets the proceeds, you and your spouse need a written agreement. In the agreement, one spouse transfers all interest in a particular insurance policy to the other spouse. Contact your insurance company for the proper form.

2. Children Under 18

If you want to name a minor child as a beneficiary of your life insurance policy, you need to arrange some legal means for the proceeds to be managed by a competent adult. If you don't, and the child is not yet 18

at your death, the insurance company would require that a court appoint a property guardian for the children before releasing the proceeds.
That would necessitate attorney's fees, court proceedings and court
supervision of the insurance proceeds—costs and hassles the child
surely won't benefit from. There are several ways to prevent this.

- Instead of naming the child as beneficiary, name a trusted adult
  who will use the money for the child's benefit.

- Leave the proceeds directly to the child, but appoint an adult
  custodian to manage the money under your state's Uniform
  Transfers to Minors Act. (See Chapter 2, Section G.)

- Name your living trust (or successor trustee, depending on which
  the insurance company prefers) as the beneficiary of the policy.
  In the trust document, name the minor child as beneficiary of any
  money the trust receives from the policy. Also establish within
  the trust a method to impose adult management over the proceeds—a child's trust or a custodianship under the Uniform
  Transfers to Minors Act.

3. Your Estate

It's generally a bad idea to name your estate as a life insurance beneficiary, because it means the proceeds of the policy must go through
probate. (If you name any other beneficiary, no probate is required.)
Your estate probably won't need the cash; most estates contain enough
cash, or assets that can be sold for cash, to pay debts and taxes. And
unless life insurance proceeds are used for estate costs, they will be
distributed to someone, eventually. So it seems foolhardy to reduce the
amount inheritors receive from your life insurance because of probate
costs—or add to the time they must wait before they get the money.

■

Use Disclaimers

It may sound strange, but you may be able to reduce your family's overall estate taxes by declining to accept property that has been left to you. Turning down a gift this way is called "disclaiming" it. If you disclaim property, it goes to the alternate beneficiary named in the trust or will, or to someone who was specifically named to inherit it if you disclaimed. If no alternate was named, it goes to the residuary beneficiary (the person who gets everything not specifically left to someone else).

Disclaiming property lets you direct it to needier relations, avoiding the gift tax that would be assessed if you accepted the property and then passed it on. And because your estate is smaller, less estate tax will be owed at your death.

Unlike most methods of saving on estate tax, disclaimers are in the hands of beneficiaries; they aren't something that can be mandated before death. You have the right, under federal law, to disclaim all, or any part, of property left to you. (IRC § 2518.)

If you're the one doing the leaving, you can't count on your beneficiaries to make the disclaimers that you might want them to. What you *can* do is make sure your major beneficiaries know that disclaimers are an option, one that might benefit the family as a whole in certain circumstances.

A. How Disclaimers Save on Estate and Gift Tax

If you disclaim part or all of what has been left to you, it doesn't affect the estate tax owed by the deceased person's estate one bit. The estate or gift tax benefit goes, eventually, to you. Here's how.

Under federal tax law, any property you disclaim is never legally owned by you. That means it won't be included in your taxable estate at death. In addition, no gift tax is assessed against you—even though, in effect, you're giving it to someone else—again because you never owned it.

Disclaimers are particularly useful when the you don't really need the money, and accepting it would significantly increase your eventual estate tax. If the alternate beneficiary is less wealthy, then a disclaimer can reduce overall estate tax. This is often the case when the alternate beneficiary is much younger than you are.

Example: *Barton dies in 2003 and leaves his estate of $700,000 to his sister Elizabeth, who is in her 70s and has, herself, assets worth $800,000. The alternate beneficiaries of Barton's estate are Elizabeth's two children, both in their 30s, with very little property.*

If Elizabeth accepts the gift, her estate will total $1.5 million. If she then dies in the year 2006, when the estate tax exemption will be $1 million, the tax bill will be $215,000. If Elizabeth instead disclaims the gift, the property will be shared by her two children. Then, if she dies in 2006 (still owning $800,000 worth of property), no estate tax will be due.

Disclaimers can also save on gift tax. If you inherit something and then give it away, you'll be assessed gift tax if the gift is worth more than $10,000 per recipient. But a disclaimer can channel it to the person you had in mind, with no gift tax whatsoever.

Example 1: *Tony, a bachelor, leaves his entire estate to his two nephews, Phil and Angelo, in equal shares. Each is the alternate beneficiary for the other's gift.*

Among the assets at Tony's death is a beachfront vacation home. Phil, who is already financially comfortable, prefers the mountains. Angelo, on the other hand, is not as well-off financially and has vacationed every summer of his life at the beach cottage. Phil disclaims his half-interest in the beach property, in effect giving it to Angelo without paying any gift tax.

Example 2: *Babette leaves her house to her three children, in equal shares. Her living trust provides that the alternate beneficiaries for each child's share are his or her children. When Babette dies, all three of her children are quite well off. Two of them accept their share of the house. The third, Fritz, disclaims his share, deciding it's wiser to let it pass to his children, who are in their early 20s and starting their careers. Fritz knows his children will find some security in the financial nest egg his disclaimer provides.*

If Babette had specified that the alternate beneficiaries for the house were her other children, Fritz would not have disclaimed his share. He would not have wanted that share divided between his brother and sister, bringing no benefit to his children.

B. Other Benefits of Disclaimers

Wholly apart from the tax considerations, disclaimers let beneficiaries make adjustments regarding who gets what. They may want to equalize their financial positions. Or they may want to avoid the problems inherent in owning a house, business or other property together.

Example: *Sven, who's doing well in business, makes a will that leaves $200,000 each to his three children and the rest of his estate to his spouse. Later, after some business setbacks and an extended illness, his wealth has dwindled. When Sven dies, there will be almost nothing left for his widow if the $600,000 is given to his children. The children disclaim their inheritance so the money will go to their mother.*

It would have been wiser, of course, for Sven to rewrite his estate plan after his business reversals, simply leaving all his property to his wife. If the children hadn't been willing to give up their inheritances, the mother would have been out of luck.

C. IRS Rules for Disclaimers

Federal law requires that a disclaimer must meet certain rules. (IRC § 2518.) If it doesn't, you will not avoid legal ownership of the property for estate tax purposes, and what may be the main goal of the disclaimer will be lost. The IRS requirements, each of which is discussed in more detail below, are:

- The disclaimer must be in writing.

- An adult must complete a disclaimer within nine months of the death of the person leaving the property.

- A minor has until nine months after reaching age 21 to disclaim.

- You may not accept any benefit from the property before disclaiming it. (An exception exists for a surviving spouse. See Section D, below).

- You may not direct where the property you disclaim then goes. The original will or trust document (or, if there is neither, state law) determines who receives the disclaimed property.

- Joint tenancy property usually cannot be disclaimed.

1. Putting the Disclaimer in Writing

If you want to disclaim inherited property—for whatever reason and whatever the type of property—you are responsible for putting the disclaimer in writing. You must deliver the written, signed disclaimer to whoever is in control of the property at that time. This is usually the successor trustee of a living trust or the executor (personal representative) of a will.

Example: *In her living trust, Charlotte leaves one money market account to her son, Francisco, and another of roughly equal value to her daughter, Eva. The trust document provides that if either child dies before Charlotte does, the money goes to the other. She names Francisco as successor trustee of her trust.*

At Charlotte's death, Eva has plenty of money, but Francisco is struggling financially. Eva is also aware of the fact that her mother spent a large amount on her college and graduate education, while Francisco chose not to go to college. She wishes to disclaim so he can receive the money directly from Charlotte's estate without it being a taxable gift from her.

As successor trustee, Francisco is bound by law to follow the directions in his mother's trust. If Eva just calls him up and tells him to take her money, he can't legally do it. He needs a written disclaimer so he can follow the trust instructions and satisfy IRS regulations. Only when armed with the signed disclaimer from Eva will he have the power to change his mother's primary instructions and take the money himself. (See Section 4, below, covering complexities that can arise when a trustee of a living trust disclaims trust property.)

2. The Nine-Month Deadline

IRS rules require that an adult who wishes to disclaim must do so within nine months of the death of the original giver—that is, the person who created the trust or wrote the will. The nine-month period allows some time for survivors to begin getting back on their feet emotionally and to get the information they need to make wise financial decisions.

Example: *Makoto dies suddenly in 2002, leaving a wife, Rose, in her 60s and two adult children. His will leaves everything to Rose or, if she doesn't survive him, to the children. Makoto's elder son, Keiji, who is executor of the will, sees immediately that the estate is worth about $1.5 million, more than Rose, who has substantial assets of her own, needs. When Keiji hires a lawyer to probate the will, the lawyer advises changing things around for tax purposes. But no one in the family wants to think about these issues so soon after Makoto's death.*

The nine-month period gives the attorney time to draft a tax-savings plan and explain it to the family. Also, the family has a chance to look at the situation and assess who needs what, and when.

In the end, Rose decides to disclaim $700,000, the amount of the personal exemption in 2002. The $700,000 goes to the children, free of estate tax. Now Rose inherits only $800,000. Her total estate is smaller than if she'd inherited the $1.5 million, so the estate tax due at her death will be lower. But Rose isn't motivated only by tax savings. She wants her children to have this money now, when they are working hard and raising their own children. With the disclaimer they get her help, with no taxable gift having been made by Rose.

DISCLAIMERS BY MINORS

A minor can disclaim a gift within nine months of becoming age 21. This rule raises some big questions. Who manages the property until the minor turns 21? What can be done with it? Who may benefit from the property during this time? The answers, which can be complicated, depend on state law. If you are the parent or guardian of a minor who has been left property and who may want to disclaim it, seek some good professional advice.

3. Benefit From Disclaimed Property

Unless you are disclaiming property inherited from your spouse (see Section D, below), you cannot use or accept any benefit from the property, however brief the use or slight the benefit. For example, if you receive rent from gift real estate for a short time and then decide you want to disclaim the entire gift, it's too late. The disclaimer will not be valid for estate tax purposes.

Receiving a benefit after making a disclaimer also invalidates the disclaimer for tax purposes. For example, you cannot disclaim property that then goes into a trust that pays you, or even could pay you, any income.

Example: *Brennan disclaims the $100,000 his father left him. His disclaimer sends the money to the alternate beneficiary—a family trust with five potential beneficiaries, including Brennan. Because Brennan is a potential beneficiary, the disclaimer is not valid for IRS purposes. The property still goes to the trust, but the transaction is considered, legally, a simple gift. Brennan will be assessed gift tax on it.*

4. Control Over Disclaimed Trust Property

In general, if you disclaim property but have the power to direct where the property will go, the disclaimer isn't valid for tax purposes. The property does go to the person chosen, but the IRS considers it a gift from you. So if the property is worth more than $10,000, you'll be assessed gift tax.

This issue can crop up if you are the successor trustee of a living trust and want to disclaim property you inherit through the trust. There's no problem if disclaimed property simply goes outright to the alternate beneficiary named in the trust document. That's the most common situation.

But if you have any power at all over the property as successor trustee of the trust, expert advice is needed. For example, if you have the power to allocate trust income among beneficiaries, the disclaimer might fail. To make the disclaimer valid, you would have to resign as trustee or decline the authority to direct distribution of the property.

Example: *Kathleen and her husband Max each create a living trust, providing that when the first spouse dies, $650,000 of his or her property will go directly into a trust for their children. Any remaining property will go outright to the surviving spouse. The surviving spouse will serve as trustee of the children's trust and will have broad authority to distribute trust principal and income to the children if they need it.*

Years later, when Max dies, the value of the couple's assets has gone way up. Estate taxes would be lower in the long run if Kathleen disclaimed the property Max left to her and let it go into the children's trust, where it would be taxed now.

But as long as she serves as trustee of the trust for the children, IRS rules prevent Kathleen from disclaiming any of the property Max left to her. That's because, as trustee, she has the authority to direct the distribution of property to the trust beneficiaries. To have a valid disclaimer, she will have to resign as trustee.

5. Disclaiming Joint Tenancy Property

It's rare that property held in joint tenancy or tenancy by the entirety can be disclaimed. (Such property goes automatically to the surviving co-owner(s) when one co-owner dies.) An IRS rule prohibits a surviving joint owner from disclaiming the inherited portion of the property unless the joint ownership was created within nine months of the death. (Treas. Reg. § 25.2518-2(c).)

Example: *Veronica and her husband Alexi have owned their home in joint tenancy for 30 years. When Alexi dies, Veronica becomes sole owner of the house. She would like to disclaim the half that had belonged to Alexi, and let it go instead to their daughter. But because the joint tenancy was created years ago, when Veronica and Alexi bought the house, she cannot.*

D. Couples and Disclaimers

Couples, whether married or not, can sometimes cut their tax bills significantly by using disclaimers.

1. Disclaiming for the Children's Benefit

Couples without a lot of money commonly write wills that leave everything to each other, naming their children as alternate beneficiaries. The plan is for the surviving mate to eventually pass everything on to the children.

But such a couple may turn out to be quite prosperous by the time one spouse dies decades after writing those simple wills. The surviving spouse's ability to disclaim part of the deceased spouse's estate, and have it go directly to their children, can achieve substantial overall estate tax savings. (A surviving spouse can also disclaim property and have it go into a trust for his or her benefit. See Section 2, below.)

Example: *While in their 40s, Boris and his wife Natasha create their estate plan, leaving all of their property to each other. Each names their three children as alternate beneficiaries. By their late 70s, together they own assets worth $900,000.*

Boris dies first, in 2002, leaving his $450,000 share to Natasha. She disclaims $200,000 of her inheritance, which means it passes directly to the children. The disclaimer allows her to receive the maximum amount possible from Boris without having her estate taxed when she dies.

Here is how the numbers look:

	Without Disclaimer —$450,000 to Natasha	*With $200,000 Disclaimer— $250,000 to Natasha*
At Boris's death in 2002:		
Boris's estate	*$450,000*	*$450,000*
Marital deduction	*($450,000)*	*-0-*
Personal exemption	*not used*	*($700,000)*
Tax due on:	*-0-*	*-0-*
At Natasha's death in 2004:		
Natasha's estate	*$900,000*	*$700,000*
Personal exemption	*($850,000)*	*($850,000)*
Tax due on:	*$50,000*	*-0-*

If Boris had died suddenly in his 50s instead of in his late 70s, Natasha might well have decided not to disclaim any of what he left her. She would have expected to live many more years, giving her plenty of time to use all of the $900,000 or explore other strategies to avoid estate tax at her death.

If you want to disclaim an interest in property you and your spouse owned together, you can disclaim only that portion left by the deceased spouse. You already own the other half of the property. (If the property is owned in joint tenancy or tenancy by the entirety, you may not be able to disclaim it at all. See Section C.5, above.)

Example: *Wyatt and Malika together own property worth $850,000. Wyatt also has well over $1 million of his own. They each leave their half of the shared property to each other, with their three children as alternate beneficiaries. After Malika dies, Wyatt wants to disclaim all he can so it will go directly to his children. He can disclaim only Malika's one-half share of their shared property, a total of $425,000. He cannot disclaim his own half share of that property, because Malika didn't leave it to him—he owned it all along.*

2. Disclaimers and AB Trusts

A surviving spouse, unlike all other beneficiaries, is allowed to receive some benefits from a disclaimed gift without invalidating the disclaimer in the eyes of the IRS. This makes possible some flexible estate planning.

One strategy is to arrange things so that if a surviving spouse disclaims money inherited from the other, it goes into an AB trust, with the surviving spouse as life beneficiary. That spouse can be given rights to receive income from the trust, spend the principal for health care and other basic needs and make use of the trust property. When the second spouse dies, the trust assets go to the couple's children or other named beneficiaries. The IRS never considers the second spouse the legal owner of the disclaimed property. (See Chapter 4.)

Example: *Bill and Esther, both in their 40s, own shared property worth $800,000. In their estate plan, each leaves their property outright to the other.*

However, they expect to acquire considerably more valuable property in the years to come. If that happens, an AB trust might be desirable to avoid owing substantial estate tax when the surviving spouse dies. On the other hand, the surviving spouse may need or want the entire estate, not just the right to get trust income or limited rights to spend principal, as an AB trust would provide. How can Bill and Esther decide now what's wisest? They don't have to.

Each leaves his or her property to the other, with the provision that any amount disclaimed will go into an AB trust. Their total estate is worth $2 million when Esther dies in 2010. Bill decides that his own estate of $1 million plus the income from Esther's $1 million is plenty. So he disclaims his inheritance from Esther, which now goes into her AB trust. Because the personal estate tax exemption is $1 million in 2010, no tax will be due at Esther's death or (unless his estate grows) at Bill's. By using the disclaimer, both estates take advantage of their personal estate tax exemptions, saving a significant amount in estate tax and leaving more, eventually, to the children.

3. Equalizing Each Spouse's Estate

When spouses own unequal amounts of property, disclaimers can be used to place assets where it's wisest for estate tax purposes. The goal is to equalize the value of both spouses' estates, or at least make them closer in size. One reason for this is that larger estates are taxed at higher rates than smaller ones. So, for example, if one spouse has an estate of $3 million, and the other has nothing, the total estate tax paid will be more than if each spouse owned $1.5 million. And if one spouse's estate is worth less than the amount of the estate tax exemption, part of that exemption is wasted.

Disclaimers used to equalize, or balance, spouses' estates are often used in combination with other estate tax-saving devices, such as AB trusts or QTIP trusts.

Example: *Sixty-year-old Guido is much wealthier than his second wife, Camilla. Guido's assets total $4 million, and Camilla's financial worth is negligible. Guido wants to ensure that Camilla is taken care of in case he dies first, but he wants his estate to eventually pass to the children of his first marriage.*

He creates a plan that will pay income to Camilla from two trusts, one a formula AB trust containing property worth the amount of the personal exemption in the year of death, and the other a QTIP trust consisting of his other assets. (Tax on property in a QTIP trust is deferred until the second spouse dies. See Chapter 5.) Guido directs that the income and then the principal of the QTIP trust be used up, if necessary, before paying Camilla income from the AB trust. At Camilla's death, the assets remaining in both trusts will go to Guido's children.

If Camilla disclaims any of the QTIP trust property, it will go into the AB trust. She remains entitled to receive the income from that trust if she needs it. However, the amount in the AB trust is subject to tax at Guido's death. Property in the QTIP trust will be subject to estate tax at Camilla's death.

Guido dies in 2008, when the estate tax exemption is $1 million. Here's what happens to his $4 million estate, with and without a $1 million disclaimer by Camilla.

	Without Disclaimer	*With $1 Million Disclaimer by Camilla*
Amount in AB trust	*$1 million*	*$2 million*
Amount in QTIP trust	*$3 million*	*$2 million*
Estate tax due at Guido's death	*-0-* *(because of marital deduction and personal exemption)*	*$345,800* *(tax on $1 million of AB trust property)*
Value of Camilla's estate	*$3 million*	*$2 million*
Estate tax due at Camilla's death	*$945,000*	*$345,800*
Total estate tax paid	*$945,000*	*$691,600*

Without a disclaimer, there is no tax at Guido's death. His estate's $1 million personal exemption takes care of the $1 million in the AB trust, and the marital deduction means the QTIP assets aren't taxed at Guido's death. If Camilla disclaims $1 million, shunting it to the AB trust, Guido's taxable estate is increased by $1 million. But because the disclaimer reduces the size of Camilla's estate, after her death overall estate taxes are cut by $253,400.

Greater savings are waiting in the wings. A smart trustee can fund the AB trust with what promise to be high-growth assets. If these assets do grow significantly in value during Camilla's life, the increase in value will not be taxed at her death. It will pass to the children free of estate tax.

At the same time, the property in the QTIP trust can be converted to high-yield assets, providing comfortable support for Camilla.

E. Planning for Disclaimers

You don't have to authorize disclaimers of property you leave, and you can't legally prohibit them. So why should you even give them a second thought when you're writing your own will or trust? Because you may want to let your beneficiaries, successor trustee and executor know that you think disclaimers may be desirable. That way, a beneficiary who wants to make a disclaimer doesn't have to worry about going against your wishes.

There are a couple of ways to go about this. One is to include a brief letter or note in the envelope with your will or living trust. It will alert the executor or successor trustee, who can in turn notify beneficiaries. You may want to suggest that the trustee consult a tax advisor before distributing any of your property.

Another way is to incorporate some specific provisions in your living trust or will, in anticipation of disclaimers. For example, if you wouldn't want a disclaimed gift to go, the alternate beneficiary, you can specify that someone else receive it. This might be true if the alternate beneficiary is likely to be in the same financial position as the primary beneficiary, as can be the case with husband and wife.

Example: *Chang, a widower, leaves his $300,000 estate to his son Tai, with Tai's wife, Claudia, as the alternate beneficiary. But Chang also provides in his living trust document that should Tai disclaim any property, it then goes to Chang's favorite nephew. When Chang dies, Tai's and Claudia's assets are quite large; neither needs the inheritance. By contrast, the nephew, who is just starting out in business, really needs the money. Tai disclaims the gift, and the $300,000 goes directly to the nephew.*

Because Tai never owns the property, his own estate is not increased for estate tax purposes. Nor has he made a taxable gift by disclaiming the gift and letting it go to Chang's nephew.

If Tai had accepted the gift, he could remove it from his estate by giving it to the nephew. He would be assessed gift tax on $290,000, the taxable portion of the gift.

■

CHAPTER 9

Use Special Rules for Small Businesses

Many family business owners dread estate taxes. The problem stems from the nature of a business—no matter how valuable, it is not a liquid asset. The people who inherit it may have trouble raising cash to pay estate tax, unless they sell the business. Happily, owners can use a number of legal methods to reduce, avoid or spread out estate taxes on a family business.

 Don't go it alone. *Good estate planning for the small business owner requires the assistance of an attorney experienced in the field.*

A. The New $1.3 Million Estate Tax Exemption

Roughly 80% of all U.S. businesses are family-owned, and the second generation takes over about 30% of them. If you meet some fairly stringent rules and qualify as an honest-to-goodness family business, you may not have to worry about estate taxes at all. That's because $1.3 million of an estate that includes a family business or farm can now pass free of estate tax.

This $1.3 million exemption is a combination of the personal estate tax exemption and an additional family business tax exemption, as shown below. It is intended to prevent families from having to sell businesses in order to raise cash to pay estate tax.

THE SPECIAL ESTATE TAX EXEMPTION FOR FAMILY BUSINESSES

Year	Personal Exemption	Additional Family Business Exemption	Total Exemption All Years
1999	$650,000	$650,000	
2000-2001	$675,000	$625,000	
2002-2003	$700,000	$600,000	$1.3 million
2004	$850,000	$450,000	
2005	$950,000	$350,000	
2006 and after	$1 million	$300,000	

The family business exemption law contains a long list of requirements designed to ensure that it is not abused. (IRC § 2033A.) In fact, there are so many requirements that many businesses won't qualify. Here are the major rules:

- **Ownership.** A 50% interest in the business must be owned by one family, or 70% by two or 90% by three. If more than one family owns the business, the family seeking the business exemption must own at least 30%.

- **Business Value.** The business's worth must exceed 50% of the value of the gross estate. The value of the business, for purposes of this requirement, doesn't include passive investment assets, excess cash or marketable securities. For example, if 25% of the value of the business consists of stocks sold on the New York Stock Exchange, only 75% of the value can be used to determine whether or not the business is more than half of the estate. The rationale is that if the business owns liquid assets, those assets can be used to pay estate tax.

- **Participation in Business.** The deceased person or members of his or her family must have owned and materially participated in the business for at least five of the eight years preceding the death.

- **No Public Trading.** The business cannot have been publicly traded within the past three years. This means that no business that's listed on a recognized stock exchange is eligible for this exemption. This won't be a hurdle for small family businesses.

- **Qualified Inheritors.** The special tax treatment is available only if the business is inherited by family members, or by employees who have worked for the business for at least 10 years before the death. For purposes of the law, a family member is the deceased person's spouse, ancestor or lineal descendant (child, grandchild and so on). A lineal descendant of the deceased person's spouse or parents, or the spouse of any lineal descendant, also qualifies.

- **Participation by Qualified Inheritor.** A qualified inheritor must materially participate in the business for at least five out of any eight-year period during the ten years following the deceased person's death.

- **Disposal of Interest.** If an inheritor sells or gives away his or her interest in the business, or ceases to materially participate in it, the estate tax that would have been due but for the special business exemption must be paid to the IRS. This is called "recapture" of the tax. If the tax is recaptured in the first six years, the whole tax break must be repaid. In years 7 to 10, a sliding scale applies. The sale of inventory or equipment, such as crops or vehicles, doesn't trigger recapture of the tax.

If a business meets all these requirements, there can be no doubt that it's a genuine multi-generational family enterprise—and deserving of family business tax treatment.

B. Special Rules for Valuing Business Real Estate

If real estate makes up a big portion of your estate, its valuation for tax purposes can have an important effect on estate taxes. A special valuation rule for the property can provide a real break for family businesses.

Real estate used in a family business or farm can be valued, for estate tax purposes, based on its present use, not its "highest and best" use. (IRC § 2032A.) This most often comes into play with farmland.

Example: *The Rutherford family farm is worth about $500 an acre as it is currently used. But suburban sprawl is fast approaching, and the family could probably get three or four times that amount if they sold out to a developer. When the eldest Rutherford dies and leaves the farm to his children, who intend to keep farming, the estate tax owed will be based on the value of the farmland as it's currently used. The IRS won't be able to argue that the land is really worth much more.*

The value of real estate can be reduced up to a maximum of $750,000 under this rule. The $750,000 figure will be indexed to changes in the cost of living beginning in 1999.

Several requirements must be met for the rule to apply:

- The value of the family business or farm must be at least 50% of the overall estate.
- The value of the business's real estate must be at least 25% of the overall estate.
- The owner must leave the family business to a family member— spouse, parents, children, grandchildren, nieces, nephews and so on.
- The deceased owner or a family member must have used the real estate for the business in five of the eight years preceding the death.

- For ten years (in some cases, 15 years) after the estate tax break, the family must notify the IRS if the property is sold or no longer used for the business. If ownership or use of the real estate changes, the new owners may be required to pay some or all of the estate tax that was previously avoided.

C. Gifts of Minority Interests in the Business

If you want your children or grandchildren to inherit your business, consider giving parts of it to them while you're still alive. Especially if the value of the business is likely to go up, this strategy could save a bundle on estate tax.

Once you give away part ownership in your business, you can't get it back—a serious consideration, of course. But depending on how your business is organized, you don't have to give up any control over the business. The trick is to give away only "minority interests" in the business. Obviously, if you keep a majority interest, you also keep control. For example, you could give away up to 49% of the voting shares of a corporation without losing exclusive control over it.

You can give away interests in your business whether it's organized as a sole proprietorship, general partnership, limited partnership, corporation or limited liability company. But as a practical matter, gifts of minority interests work only if your business is incorporated or is a family limited partnership (FLP). If you operate a sole proprietorship or general partnership, giving part ownership to your children would make them business partners, with management authority—something you may not want.

Making gifts of minority interests in your business offers two tax breaks. First, the value of what you give away is removed from your estate. Second, the value of the gift, for gift tax purposes, gets what's called a "valuation discount." This tax break can offer big savings and has become a popular way for small business owners to transfer part interests of their businesses to the next generation.

1. How the Tax Break Works

You can get a tax break when you give away minority interests—in other words, chunks of less than 50% of the voting power of the business. For gift tax purposes, the value of a minority interest in a business is worth far less than it would be if it were part of majority control of the business. This is the "valuation discount."

Two separate discounts are involved:

- **Discount for minority interest.** Minority owners do not have voting control over the business; they cannot manage the business, compel its sale or liquidation or distribute money to owners. So outside buyers will not pay the same price for minority interests as for majority ones.

- **Discount for lack of marketability.** A greater discount is allowed if the basic small business agreement (corporate bylaws or LLC members' agreement) restricts ownership to family members or another narrow group, as many family businesses do. In this situation, the interest cannot simply be sold to any willing buyer.

In practice, the two combined discounts can range from 20% to 50%, meaning that the value of the gift of the business interest can be discounted by this much. No statutes or IRS regulations govern how valuation discounts are determined, so calculating them is not easy. But a 1995 Tax Court decision (*Bernard Mendelbaum v. Commissioner*, TC Memo 1995-255) did set out ten factors to take into account when deciding on an appropriate discount:

1. Whether or not the stock has been traded publicly.
2. Financial statement analysis (best done by an experienced tax pro, mainly to see how profitable the business is; if only average or marginal, a larger discount can be taken).

3. Dividend policy of the business (not important to most small corporations, which don't pay dividends).

4. Nature, history and industry position of the business (how well the business can compete).

5. Strength of company management (strong management increases the value of a business).

6. Degree of control in the transferred shares (if you keep control of the business, large discounts can be justified).

7. Stock transfer restrictions (the marketability limits discussed above).

8. Required holding period of stock (another stock transfer restriction).

9. Stock redemption policy of the company (if the business has not historically redeemed shareholders' stock, a larger minority discount is justified).

10. Public offering costs.

Obviously, you're going to need expert help with this kind of strategy, probably from a CPA and a lawyer. You'll need someone both to value the business (not easy in itself) and to help you figure out a fair discount that the IRS will consider reasonable.

Example: *McWilson is the sole owner of the DaaDee Corporation, which has 50,000 shares of stock. By the best estimate of McWilson and his accountant, if the whole business—all the shares—were sold, the value would be $2 million. So, at first glance, each share is worth $40. But if the shares are split between minority and majority shareholders, the minority shares are worth less.*

McWilson gives 10,000 shares to each of his two daughters. (In his living trust, he leaves the rest to them equally.) For gift tax purposes, he values the minority shares at $30, a 25% discount. Realistically, each share transfers $40 worth of assets; after all, each daughter will eventually own 50% of the *business, and there won't be any distinction then between majority and minority shares.*

If the value of the discounted portion of a family business you give away exceeds the annual gift tax exempt amount (currently $10,000), you must file a federal gift tax return. (See Chapter 1.) On the return, you must disclose the size of the discount and explain how you arrived at it.

2. Family Limited Partnerships and Valuation Discounts

"Family limited partnerships" (FLPs) have been heavily promoted recently as tools for reducing estate tax. It's true that they can be a handy structure for giving away discounted minority interests, but they are not a magic way to avoid taxes.

Every limited partnership has active owners (usually called managing or general partners) and passive or limited partners. In a typical family limited partnership, parents form an FLP and transfer an existing business to it. The parents are the general partners, who have management authority and liability for partnership debts. Children are limited partners, and are treated like investors who have an ownership interest in—but no right to manage—the business. Limited partners are liable for debts of the business only up to the amount of money they have put into it. They can also work in the business and earn wages, but they don't have to.

Example: *Dave and Andrea run an antique business. They have never bothered with formal ownership papers, but they pay taxes as a sole proprietorship (married couples can do that). When they reach their late 60s, they form a family limited partnership and start giving each of their two grown children a percentage interest in the business. They make sure that, taking into account the valuation discount, their yearly gift to each child is worth less than $20,000. That way, each gift is less than Dave and Andrea's combined*

$20,000 annual gift tax exemption ($10,000 per recipient per year), so no gift tax is assessed.

The children are limited partners and have no say in the day-to-day affairs of the business. In several years, Dave and Andrea have transferred 48% of their business to their kids, tax-free, while keeping control of its management.

⚠ Phony businesses don't fool the IRS. *Any business, including a family business, can be organized as a limited partnership. However, creating a family limited partnerships for a vacation home or investment portfolio won't work, even though you manage the assets for profit. The IRS has refused to accept valuation discounts unless what they consider a legitimate business is involved. Currently the IRS is aggressively litigating a series of cases, claiming the family businesses are shams. It's not likely to be in your family's interests to be on the cutting edge of this fight.*

Lawsuits now in progress between the IRS and various inventive givers (and their sly estate tax advisers) should help define what is a valid family business. Some extremes are already clear. A family "business" created a few days before death, for the sole purpose of reducing estate taxes, does not qualify as a valid business for tax purposes. Also, the business must be run independently, separate from the owner's personal finances.

💼 Choosing a legal structure for your business. *If you want to explore creating a family limited partnership for estate planning purposes, see an experienced lawyer. And keep in mind that many factors should influence your choice of how to organize your business. Estate planning options are just one part of the picture.*

D. Deferring Estate Tax Payments

If, despite your best efforts, estate tax is due after your death, there's still some good news: The tax payments can be spread out for a long time. If a family business or farm is part of a taxable estate, estate tax can be paid over a period of years, rather than within nine months of the owner's death as otherwise required.

The basic rule is that estate tax assessed against the value of a small business or family farm can be deferred for five years and then paid in up to ten annual installments. (IRC § 6166.) In other words, the final payment isn't due until 15 years after the owner's death. To qualify for this special treatment, the value of the small business must exceed 35% of the total estate.

Example: *Andrew, the owner of Shortstop Shipping, dies in 2003. The business has a net worth of $2.6 million, and the total net value of his estate is $3.8 million. Under the combined family business and personal estate tax exemptions, $1.3 million can pass free from estate tax. The remaining $2.5 million is taxable. The taxes due are postponed for five years, then paid off over the next ten.*

This option is available for partnerships that have 15 or fewer partners, and corporations with 15 or fewer shareholders. For corporations, at least 20% of the voting stock must be included in the gross estate of the deceased owner.

Interest must be paid on the unpaid taxes each year. Currently, the rate is a rock-bottom 2% on the tax attributable to the first $1 million of the taxable value of the business. (That rate applies to deaths after December 31, 1997; see Rev. Proc. 98-15.) And if the new owners sell more than 50% of the business to a non-family member, the tax becomes due immediately.

OTHER ESTATE PLANNING ISSUES FOR SMALL BUSINESS OWNERS

The death of the sole or part owner of a small business is likely to seriously disrupt that business. If no planning has been done, the disruption can be catastrophic, sometimes resulting in the failure of the business. You need to have a sound succession plan.

Dealing With Co-Owners. If you share ownership of a business, you must consider the rights of the other owners. These rights are usually spelled out in a partnership agreement, corporate bylaws or shareholders' agreement, or the operating agreement of a limited liability company. Some agreements require the surviving owners to buy out a deceased owners' share; others simply give them the option to do so. One standard provision gives surviving owners a "right of first refusal," allowing them to buy the interest for the price offered by an outside would-be purchaser. If there is no outside offer, another provision may provide a method for determining the value of the deceased owner's interest in the business.

In the absence of an owners' agreement, the rights of the surviving owners are determined by state law. It's much better, of course, to work out an agreement beforehand.

Ensuring Continuity. Even if you expect your heirs to sell your business, you'll want them to have some flexibility in the timing of the sale. It's rarely desirable to sell a business immediately after the death of its owner.

One way to achieve at least short-term continuity is for key employees to agree, in writing, that they will stay around for a while after the owner's death, perhaps in exchange for a portion of the eventual sale proceeds. Or you could incorporate the business and make key employees officers of the corporation and minority stockholders, perhaps through a stock option plan. Employees are less likely to quit if they have an ownership interest in the business.

Avoiding Probate. It can be disastrous for a small business to become enmeshed in probate. Not only is probate costly, but worse, it ties up the business under court control for months or longer. For a number of tax and ownership reasons, a living trust is usually the best choice to avoid probate of your business. Living trusts work well for both solely owned businesses and businesses you own with others. Your partnership agreement, corporate bylaws or shareholders' agreement or LLC operating agreement should specifically permit you to transfer your interest to a living trust. If it doesn't, revise it.

Tax Savvy for Small Business, *by Fred Daily, thoroughly covers tax issues of importance to every family business owner.*

Buy-Sell Agreements, *by Anthony Mancuso and Beth Laurence, explains several IRS-approved methods of valuing business interests.*

Form Your Own Limited Liability Company, *by Anthony Mancuso, shows you how to create a members' operating agreement that covers sale, valuation and succession issues.*

How to Form Your Own Corporation, *by Anthony Mancuso (California, New York, Texas or Florida edition), explains the nuts and bolts of forming a corporation, including drafting shareholders' agreements that cover buy-out issues.*

The Partnership Book, *by Denis Clifford and Ralph Warner, explains how business partners can write an agreement to cover sale and valuation issues.*

Make Your Own Living Trust, *by Denis Clifford, contains all the forms and instructions you need to create a living trust to avoid probate of your assets, including a business.*

Living Trust Maker *software lets you create a valid probate-avoidance living trust with your personal computer.*

All of these books and software are published by Nolo Press.

■

GLOSSARY

For definitions of many more legal terms, see SharkTalk, Nolo's online legal dictionary, at www.nolo.com.

AB trust: A kind of bypass trust used by couples who want to save on estate tax. The surviving spouse is the *life beneficiary* of most or all of the deceased spouse's property; usually, the couple's children are the *final beneficiaries*. Because the surviving spouse never legally owns the trust property, it is not taxed at that spouse's death.

Affiant: Someone who signs an *affidavit*.

Affidavit: A written statement of facts that is signed under oath before a notary public.

Annual gift tax exclusion: The amount of property you can give away to any one recipient in one calendar year, free of federal gift tax. Currently, the amount is $10,000; that figure is indexed to inflation.

Annuitant: Someone who receives payments from an annuity contract.

Annuity: A contract that guarantees someone fixed payments for life.

Annuity trust: A trust that pays a beneficiary a fixed amount each year.

Appraiser: A person who is hired to determine the market value of *real estate* or other property. If you make a valuable gift to a charity, you'll need an appraiser to make a written appraisal of the property.

Appreciated property: Property that has gone up in value since you acquired it.

Assign: Transfer ownership of something to someone. For example, some people assign ownership of a life insurance policy to someone else or to a trust.

Basis: See *Tax basis.*

Beneficiary: A person or organization who inherits property under the terms of a will, trust, payable-on-death account, retirement account or life insurance policy.

Bypass trust: A trust designed to save on overall estate tax. The trust has a *life beneficiary* and *final beneficiaries*. The life beneficiary typically receives any income generated by the trust property, and may spend principal under certain circumstances if allowed by the trust document. When the life beneficiary dies, the final beneficiaries inherit the trust property outright. Because the life beneficiary was never the legal owner, the trust property is not part of his or her taxable estate. See *AB trust*.

Cash surrender value: The amount of money an insurance policy owner can get by cashing in the insurance policy with the issuing company. Only *permanent* (not *term*) insurance policies have a cash surrender value.

Charitable gift annuity: An annuity that is purchased as part of making a gift to a charity. Part of the property you transfer to the charity is simply a charitable gift, and part goes for the purchase of an *annuity* contract. You get an immediate income tax deduction, fixed payments for life and eventual estate tax savings. After your death, the charity receives outright the amount you gave (increased, it hopes, by investment over the years).

Charitable remainder trust: A kind of trust that allows you to make a gift to a charity during your life. In return, you get both annual income tax deductions and, after your death, estate tax savings.

Community property: A system of law followed in nine states (Arizona, California, Idaho, Louisiana, Nevada, New Mexico, Texas, Washington and Wisconsin). In those states, very generally, all property acquired by a couple while married is community property, except for gifts to and inheritances by one spouse only, or unless the spouses have signed an agreement to the contrary. If separate property and community property are mixed together (commingled) in a bank account and expenditures made from the account, the goods purchased are usually treated as community property unless they can be specifically linked to separate property.

Crummey trust: A complicated trust that contains provisions allowing trust beneficiaries to *disclaim* distributions every year. Typically, Crummey provisions are used in *life insurance trusts*. The beneficiaries disclaim the money every year, and that money is used to pay the premiums of the life insurance policy owned by the trust. Having the beneficiaries turn down the money results in gift tax savings.

Custodian: Someone authorized to manage property given to or inherited by a child, under laws called the *Uniform Transfers to Minors Act* or the *Uniform Gifts to Minors Act.*

Decedent: Someone who has died.

Decree: A court order.

Deed: A document that transfers ownership of a piece of real estate. There are many types of deeds, which may be used for different kinds of transfers.

Deed of trust: A special type of deed similar to a mortgage.

Disclaim: To turn down a gift authorized by a will or trust, so that it will pass to the alternate beneficiary. Disclaimers are often used to cut a family's overall estate tax bill.

Distributees: Another term for *heirs* and *beneficiaries*, or the people who receive property under the terms of a will, trust or insurance policy.

Donee: Someone who receives a gift.

Donor: Someone who gives a gift.

Encumbrance: Debt (for example, mortgage, property tax, mechanic's lien, judgment lien, deed of trust, security interest) tied to specific property as collateral.

Equity: The difference between the fair market value of your real estate and personal property and the amount you still owe on it, if any.

Estate: Generally, the property you own when you die. There are different kinds of estates, including your taxable estate (what is subject to estate tax), your probate estate (what must go through probate) and your net estate (your net worth).

Estate planning: Taking steps, while you're alive, to leave your property to your loved ones with a minimum of fuss, expense and taxes.

Estate tax: See *Federal estate and gift tax.*

Estate tax threshold: The size of an estate at which estate taxes may be due.

Executor: The person specified in a will to manage the *estate*, deal with the probate court, collect the assets and distribute them as the will has specified. If there is no will, or no executor nominated under the will, the probate court will appoint such a person, who is called the "administrator" of the estate.

Executrix: A term, now rarely used, for a female executor.

Exemption trust: A *bypass trust* that contains property worth no more than the amount that can be passed free of *estate tax*.

Fair market value: The price for which an item of property would be bought by a willing buyer and sold by a willing seller. Estates are appraised to determine their fair market value, and the result determines whether or not an estate tax return must be filed.

Family allowance: A certain amount of a deceased person's money to which immediate family members are entitled when probate proceedings are begun. The amount is determined by state law and varies greatly from state to state.

Family limited partnership: A *limited partnership* business owned and run by family members. In a typical FLP, the parents are the general partners, who have management authority and liability for business debts. Children are limited partners.

Federal gift and estate tax: A tax imposed by the federal government when someone gives away or leaves large amounts of property. Rates are the same for property given away during life or left at death. Every estate can leave $650,000 to $1 million (depending on the year of death) tax-free. In addition, property given or left to a qualified charity or to a spouse who is a U.S. citizen is not taxed.

Final beneficiary: A beneficiary of a trust who inherits trust property outright after the *life beneficiary's* interest ends.

Formula clause: A provision in a *bypass trust* that directs the trustee, at the grantor's death, to transfer to the trust as much property as can be passed tax-free under federal law in the year of the grantor's death. See *Estate tax threshold*.

Funding a trust: Transferring ownership of property to a trust. Without this step, the trust document has no effect on what happens to the property.

Future interest: An interest in property at a future time. The recipient of such an interest does not have any immediate rights to the property. Gifts of future interests do not qualify for the *annual gift tax exclusion*.

Gift: Property passed to another for nothing in return or for substantially less than its actual market value. Any gift worth more than the *annual gift tax exclusion* per year to an individual requires a gift tax return and may be subject to *federal gift and estate tax*.

Gift tax: See *Federal estate and gift tax*

Grantor: Someone who creates a trust. Also called trustor or settlor.

Gross estate: For federal estate tax filing purposes, the total of all property you own at death, without regard to any debts or liens against the property or the costs of administering the estate. However, taxes are due only on the value of the property the person actually owned.

Heir: Generally, any person who is entitled by law to inherit if an estate is not completely disposed of under a will or other valid transfer device.

Incidents of ownership: Certain rights over some kind of property—for example, the right to receive rent from a commercial building.

Inheritance tax: A tax imposed by some states on property owned by a deceased person.

Intangible personal property: Property that does not have a physical form but is represented by a document. Stock in a corporation, the right to receive a pension, patents and copyrights are all examples of intangible personal property.

Inter vivos trust: See *Living trust.*

Intestate: Someone who dies without having made a valid will is said to die "intestate." In that event, the *estate* is distributed according to the state's *intestate succession* law.

Intestate succession: The method by which property is distributed when someone fails to leave a valid will. Each state's law provides that the property be given to the closest surviving relatives. In most states, the surviving spouse, children, parents, siblings, nieces and nephews and next of kin inherit, in that order.

Irrevocable trust: A trust that cannot be changed or revoked once it becomes operational. For example, an *AB trust* becomes irrevocable when the grantor dies.

Joint tenancy: A way to hold title to jointly owned real estate or other property. When two or more people own property as joint tenants, and one of them dies, the others automatically become owners of the deceased owner's share. Because of this "right of survivorship," a joint tenancy interest in property does not go through probate.

Lien: A legal claim against property.

Life beneficiary: Someone who is entitled to certain benefits for as long as he or she lives. For example, the life beneficiary of an *AB trust* is generally entitled to receive income from trust property for life. After the life beneficiary dies, another beneficiary (often called the *final beneficiary*) receives the trust property itself.

Life estate: The rights of a *life beneficiary.*

Life insurance trust: An *irrevocable trust* that is created to own a life insurance policy.

Limited partnership: A business organized as a partnership, with both general and limited partners. General partners run the business and are liable for the business's debts. Limited partners are passive investors who have no management authority and are liable for business debts only to the extent they have invested in the business. See *Family limited partnership.*

Lineal descendant: A child, grandchild or more distant direct descendant.

Living trust: A probate-avoidance trust you create while you're alive and which remains under your control. At your death, property owned by the trust passes directly to the trust beneficiaries, free of probate. Sometimes called a lifetime or "inter vivos" (Latin for "among the living") trust.

Marital exemption: A deduction allowed by the federal estate tax laws for all property passed to a surviving spouse who is a U.S. citizen. This deduction is unlimited. A surviving spouse can inherit millions without any tax at all.

Marital life estate trust: Another name for an *AB trust* for a married couple.

Marital property: A term used in Wisconsin for certain property owned by a married couple; for practical purposes, it is the Wisconsin version of "community property."

Minor: In almost every state, any person under 18 years of age.

Net estate: The value of all property owned at death less liabilities.

Next of kin: The closest relatives (as defined by state law) of a deceased person.

Notary public: Someone authorized by state law to witness signatures on legal documents and sign them as evidence of the signature's validity.

Permanent insurance: Life insurance that can be automatically renewed, for as long as you live, without a new physical examination. Types of permanent insurance include whole life, universal life and variable life insurance.

Personal property: Any kind of property except real estate.

Personal representative: A generic title applied to an administrator or executor of an estate.

Present interest: The right to use or receive a benefit from property immediately. Only gifts of a present interest qualify for the *annual gift tax exclusion*.

Probate: Generally, the process by which: 1) the authenticity of your will, if any, is established; 2) the court authorizes your executor or administrator to act for your estate; 3) your debts and taxes are paid; 4) your heirs are identified; and 5) property in your *probate estate* is distributed according to your will or state *intestate succession* laws.

Probate estate: All the assets owned at death that require some form of court proceeding before title may be transferred to the new owners. Property that passes at death without court approval (property in a trust, life insurance proceeds or property held in *joint tenancy*, for example) is not part of the probate estate.

QDOT: A "Qualified Domestic Trust" used by married couples when one spouse is not a U.S. citizen. It allows estate tax to be postponed until the death of the second spouse.

QTIP trust: A "Qualified Terminable Interest Trust" used by married couples. It postpones estate tax until the death of the second spouse, and allows that first spouse to name *final beneficiaries* for his or her assets.

Quasi-community property: If a married couple moves to a community property state, certain property they acquired in their previous home may be considered "quasi-community property." The rules vary from state to state. Quasi-community property is treated just like community property.

Real property: Real estate. That includes land, of course, and things attached to land such as trees, crops, buildings and stationary mobile homes. Anything that is not real property is termed personal property. See *Personal property*.

Recapture: The paying back of taxes. For example, if family members who inherit a business take advantage of the special estate tax exemption available to family businesses, and then sell the business a few years later, they will owe estate tax.

Residuary estate: All the property in the probate estate except for property that is specifically and effectively left to designated beneficiaries.

Securities: Stocks and bonds.

Separate property: In community property states, all property owned by a married person that is not community or quasi-community property. Separate property generally includes all property acquired before the marriage or after a legal separation, property acquired by separate gift or inheritance at any time, property acquired from separate property funds and property that has been designated separate property by agreement of the spouses.

Settlor: Same as *grantor*.

Stepped-up basis: The tax basis of someone who inherits appreciated property. The recipient's tax basis is raised, or "stepped up," from the original basis to the property's market value at the time of the death.

Successor trustee: The person named in a trust document to take over as trustee after the death or incapacity of the original trustee.

Surviving spouse: A widow or widower.

Tax basis: The figure used to calculate taxable gain or loss when you sell an item of property. Generally, the amount of your basis is what you paid for the item or, if you inherited it, its market value at the time you acquired it. If you have a basis of $100, and sell the item for $300, you have a taxable gain of $200. See *Stepped-up basis*.

Taxable estate: Property subject to the federal gift and estate tax. It's the fair market value of all assets owned at death (gross estate) less certain allowable deductions, such as debts, last illness and funeral expenses and expenses of administering the estate.

Tenancy by the entirety: A special kind of joint tenancy that's only for married couples. It is not available in all states.

Tenancy in common: A way two or more people can own property together. Each can leave his or her interest upon death to beneficiaries of his choosing instead of to the other owners (as is the case with joint tenancy). Also unlike joint tenancy, the ownership shares need not be equal.

Term life insurance: A form of life insurance that, unlike *permanent insurance*, is not automatically renewable for your whole life and has no cash value.

Testate: Someone who dies after making a valid will is said to have died "testate."

Testator: A person who makes a will.

Transfer agent: A representative of a corporation who is authorized to handle the paperwork of transferring ownership of the corporation's stock from one person to another.

Trust: A legal entity that exists only on paper but has the ability to own property. See *Living trust, Charitable trust*.

Trustee: The person who has legal authority over assets owned by a trust. With a simple probate-avoidance trust, the person who creates the trust is also the initial trustee.

Uniform Gifts to Minors Act: A set of statutes that allows you to appoint a custodian to manage certain kinds of property you give to a minor during your life. It does not cover property left at death. It's available in all states that have not adopted the broader *Uniform Transfers to Minors Act*.

Uniform Transfer-on-Death Security Act: A statute adopted by more than 30 states that allows you to name a beneficiary to inherit your stocks or bonds without probate.

Uniform Transfers to Minors Act: A set of statutes, adopted by almost all states, which lets you appoint an adult "custodian" to manage property you give or leave to a minor.

Unitrust: A trust that pays its beneficiaries an amount equal to a percentage of the value of the trust assets each year.

Will: A document, signed and witnessed as required by law, in which you state who you want to inherit your property. A will is also the place to name a personal guardian to raise your young children if you and the other parent can't.

INDEX

NOLO IN THE NEWS

"Nolo helps lay people perform legal tasks without the aid—or fees—of lawyers."

—USA TODAY

Nolo books are ..."written in plain language, free of legal mumbo jumbo, and spiced with witty personal observations."

—ASSOCIATED PRESS

"...Nolo publications...guide people simply through the how, when, where and why of law."

—WASHINGTON POST

"Increasingly, people who are not lawyers are performing tasks usually regarded as legal work... And consumers, using books like Nolo's, do routine legal work themselves."

—NEW YORK TIMES

"...All of [Nolo's] books are easy-to-understand, are updated regularly, provide pull-out forms...and are often quite moving in their sense of compassion for the struggles of the lay reader."

—SAN FRANCISCO CHRONICLE

fold here

- -

NOLO PRESS
950 Parker Street
Berkeley, CA 94710-9867

PRESS   Attn: │ **ESTX 1.0** │